THIS DEER HUNTING LOG BOOK

BELONGS TO:

_____

DEDICATION

This Deer Hunting Log Book is dedicated to all the Deer Hunters out there who love to plan out their deer hunting activities, and document their findings in the process.

You are my inspiration for producing books and I'm honored to be a part of keeping all of your deer hunting information and records organized.

How to use this Deer Hunting Log Book:

This useful deer hunting log book is a must-have for anyone that needs to record their deer chasing activities! You will love this easy to use deer hunting log book to track and record all your hunting season activities.

Each interior page includes space to record & track the following:

Date - Write down the date of your deer hunting activity
Location - Use this space to fill in the location of the deer hunt
Time - Record the current time of the deer hunt
Weather Conditions - Fill in the weather conditions, from sunny to snowy
Hunting Type - Stay on task by writing down which type of hunter, whether its big game or elk hunting...
Co-Hunters - Record anyone who is with you on this deer hunt
Deer Target Area - Write down on this deer template of your intended target, checkmark space as to whether its male or female deer

Ammunition - Record which types of ammo are used on your deer hunting adventure
Activity and Sightings - Write down any deer sightings in the area

If you are new to hunting deer or have been at it for a while, this deer hunting log book is a must have! Can make a great useful gift for anyone that loves to go deer hunting!

Enjoy!

DATE	WEATHER CONDITIONS
TIME	
LOCATION	

HUNTING TYPE	TERRAIN LEVEL
CO-HUNTERS	EASY 1 2 3 4 5 HARD

GEAR / SETUP	TARGET AREA
AMMUNITION	♂ ♀

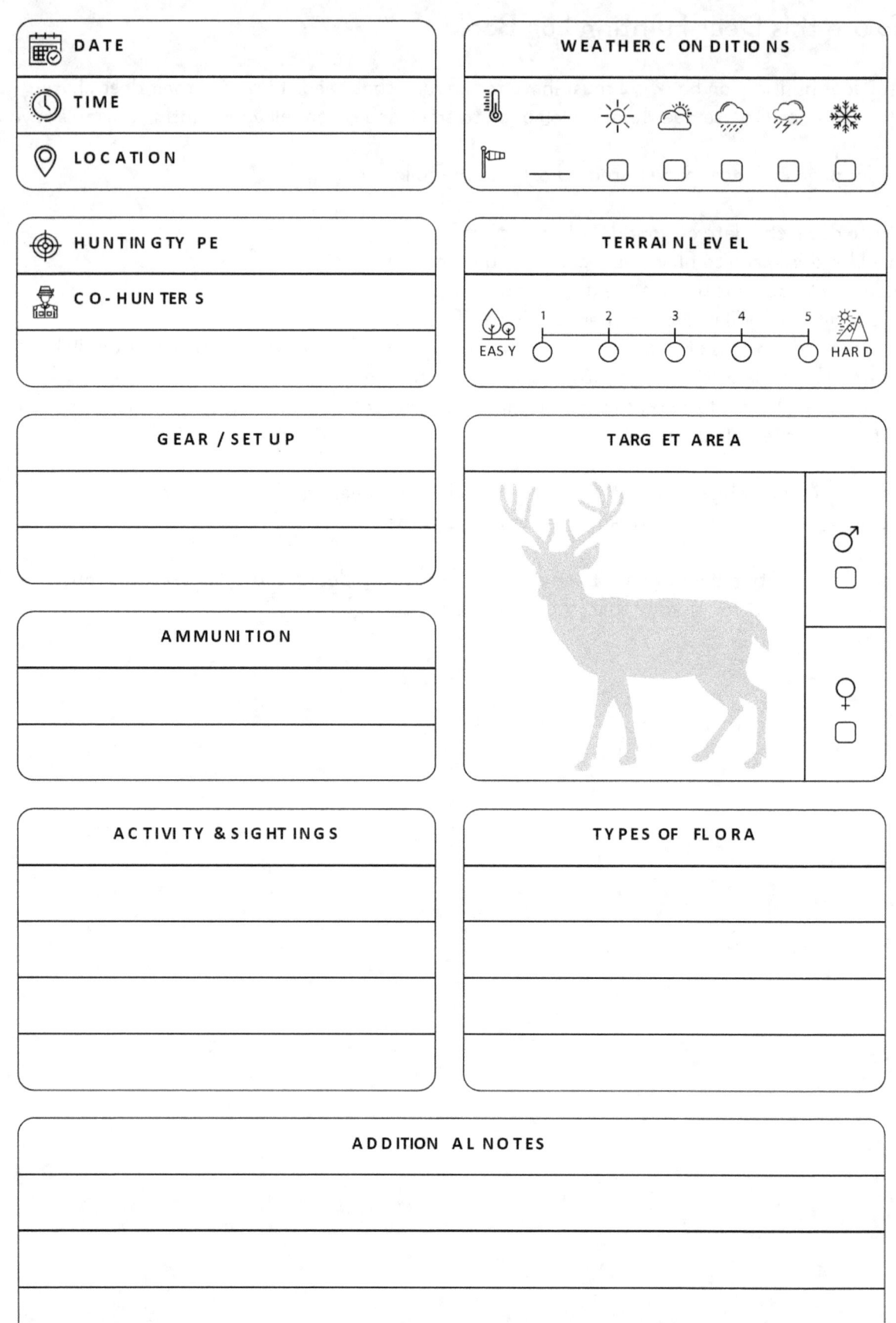

ACTIVITY & SIGHTINGS	TYPES OF FLORA

ADDITIONAL NOTES

| DATE |
| TIME |
| LOCATION |

WEATHER CONDITIONS

🌡 _____ ☀ ⛅ 🌧 ⛈ ❄
🌬 _____ ☐ ☐ ☐ ☐ ☐

| HUNTING TYPE |
| CO-HUNTERS |

TERRAIN LEVEL

EASY 1 2 3 4 5 HARD
      ○ ○ ○ ○ ○

GEAR / SETUP

TARGET AREA

♂ ☐

♀ ☐

AMMUNITION

ACTIVITY & SIGHTINGS

TYPES OF FLORA

ADDITIONAL NOTES

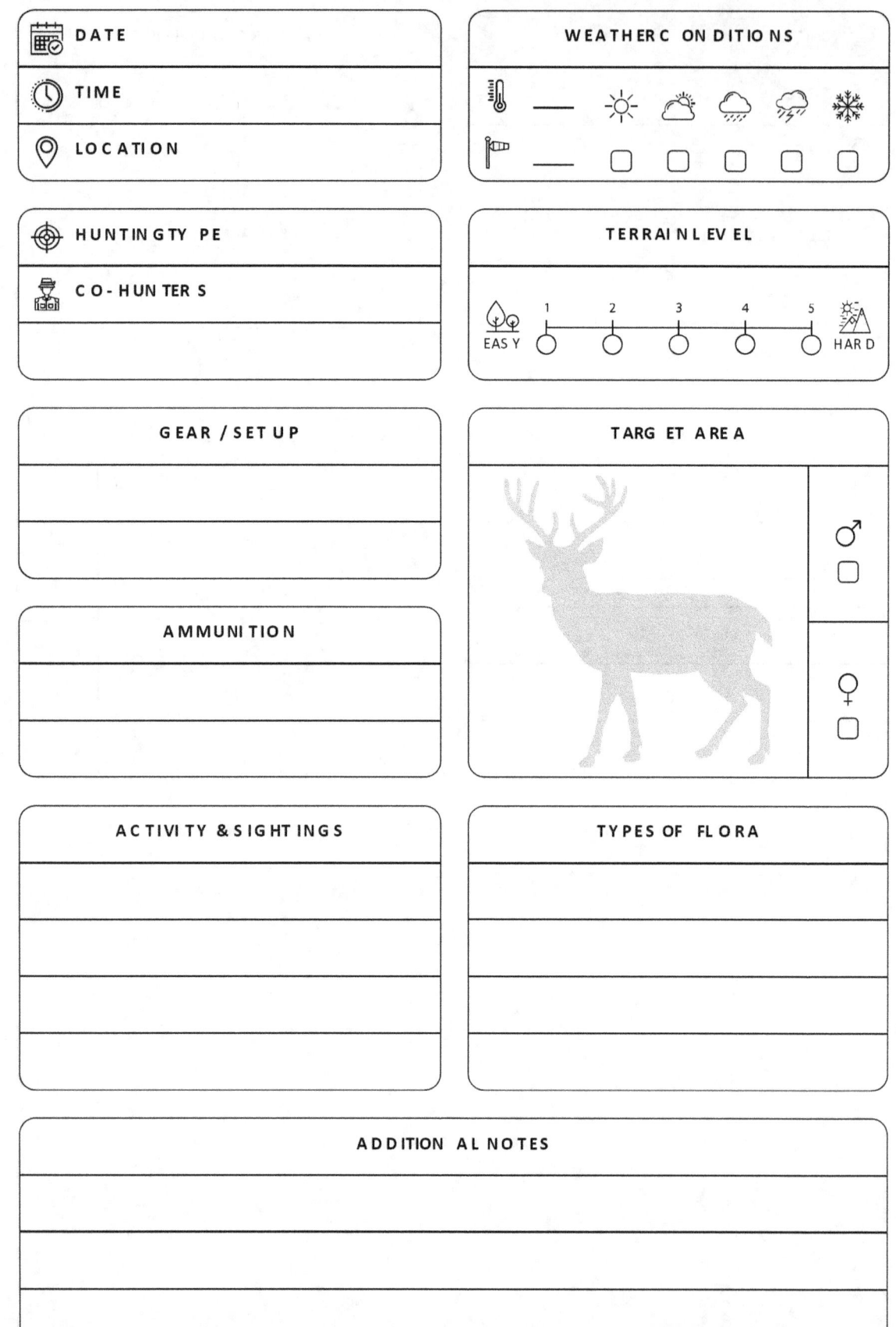

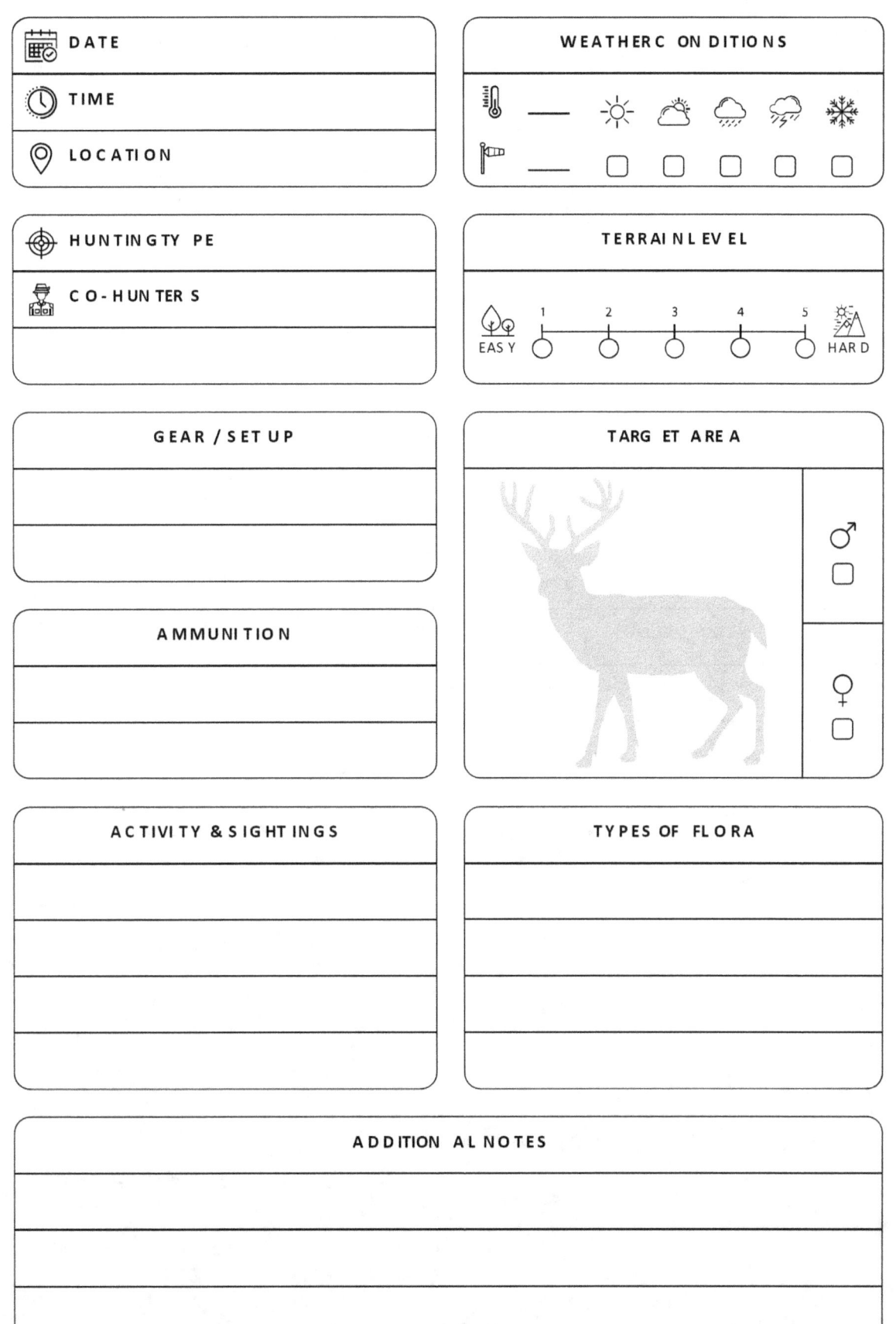

DATE	WEATHER CONDITIONS
TIME	☀️ ⛅ 🌧️ ⛈️ ❄️
LOCATION	☐ ☐ ☐ ☐ ☐

HUNTING TYPE	TERRAIN LEVEL
CO-HUNTERS	EASY 1 2 3 4 5 HARD

GEAR / SETUP

TARGET AREA

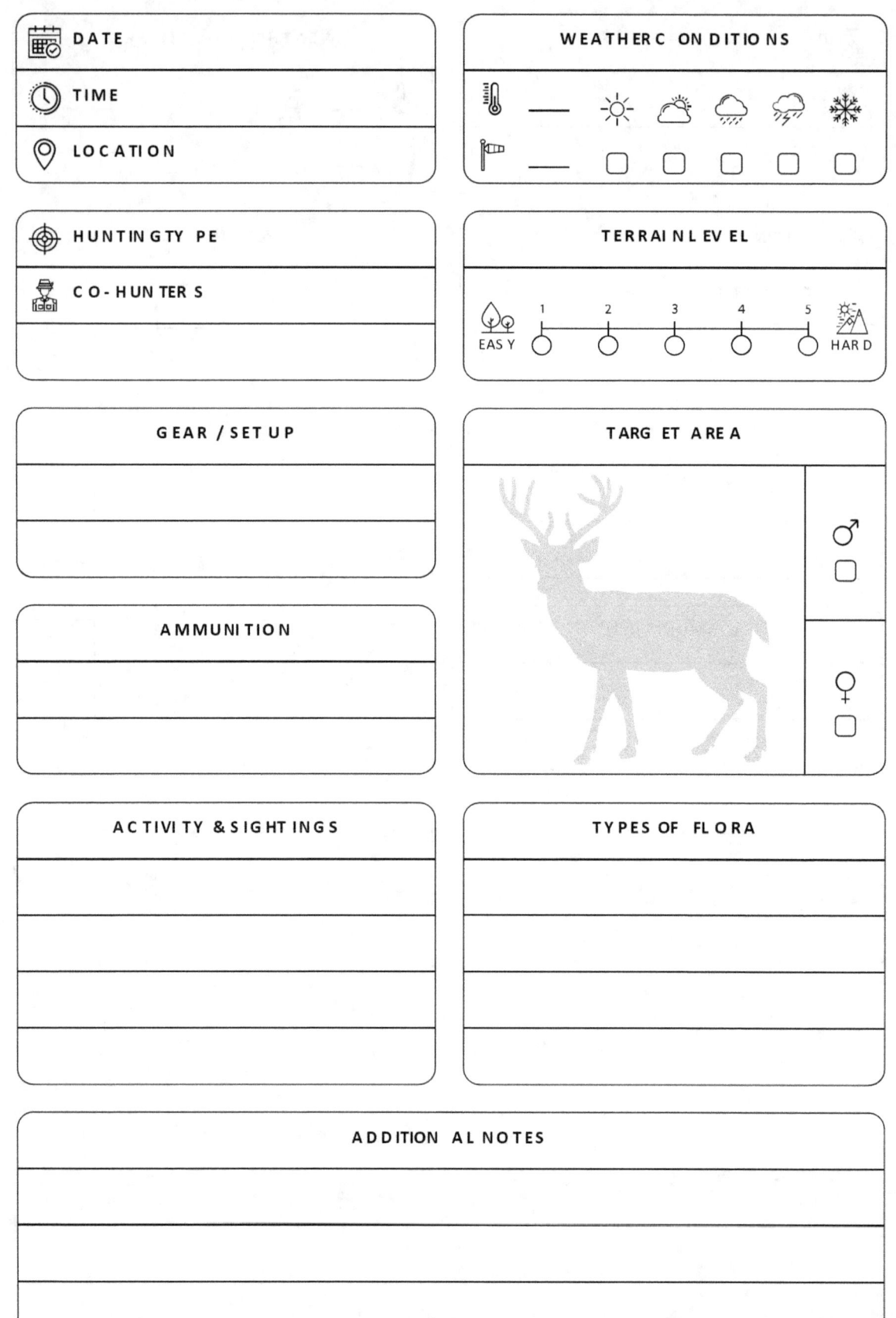

♂ ☐

♀ ☐

AMMUNITION

ACTIVITY & SIGHTINGS

TYPES OF FLORA

ADDITIONAL NOTES

DATE	WEATHER CONDITIONS
TIME	☀ ⛅ 🌧 ⛈ ❄
LOCATION	

HUNTING TYPE	TERRAIN LEVEL
CO-HUNTERS	EASY 1 — 2 — 3 — 4 — 5 HARD

GEAR / SETUP

TARGET AREA

♂ ☐

♀ ☐

AMMUNITION

ACTIVITY & SIGHTINGS

TYPES OF FLORA

ADDITIONAL NOTES

DATE	WEATHER CONDITIONS
TIME	☀️ ⛅ 🌧️ ⛈️ ❄️
LOCATION	☐ ☐ ☐ ☐ ☐

HUNTING TYPE	TERRAIN LEVEL
CO-HUNTERS	EASY 1 2 3 4 5 HARD

GEAR / SETUP

TARGET AREA

♂ ☐

♀ ☐

AMMUNITION

ACTIVITY & SIGHTINGS

TYPES OF FLORA

ADDITIONAL NOTES

DATE	WEATHER CONDITIONS
TIME	☀ ⛅ 🌧 ⛈ ❄
LOCATION	☐ ☐ ☐ ☐ ☐

HUNTING TYPE	TERRAIN LEVEL
CO-HUNTERS	EASY 1 2 3 4 5 HARD

GEAR / SETUP

TARGET AREA

♂ ☐

♀ ☐

AMMUNITION

ACTIVITY & SIGHTINGS

TYPES OF FLORA

ADDITIONAL NOTES

DATE	WEATHER CONDITIONS
TIME	
LOCATION	

HUNTING TYPE	TERRAIN LEVEL
CO-HUNTERS	EASY 1 2 3 4 5 HARD

GEAR / SETUP	TARGET AREA
AMMUNITION	♂ ♀

ACTIVITY & SIGHTINGS	TYPES OF FLORA

ADDITIONAL NOTES

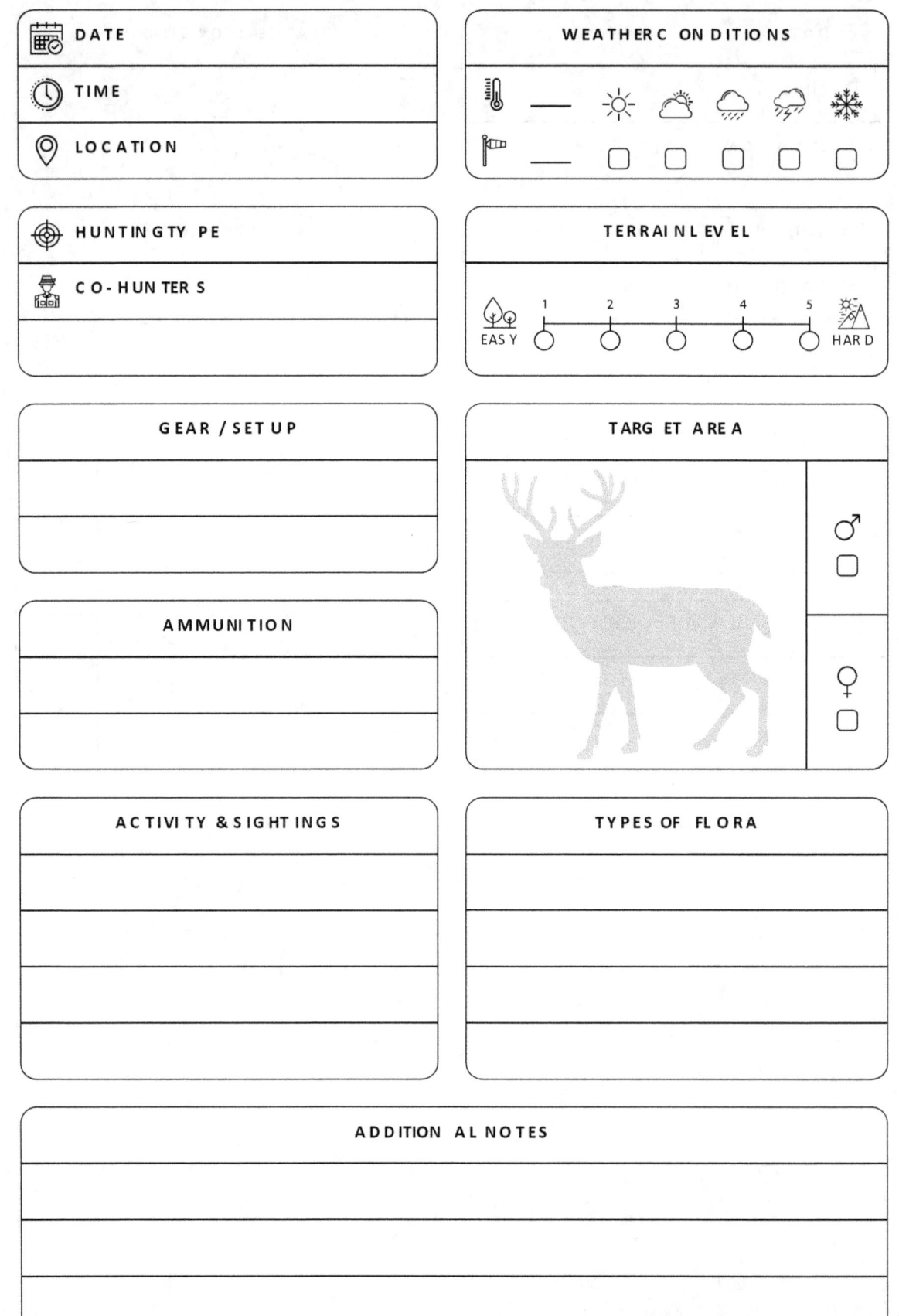

DATE

TIME

LOCATION

HUNTING TYPE

CO-HUNTERS

WEATHER CONDITIONS

TERRAIN LEVEL

1 2 3 4 5
EASY — HARD

GEAR / SETUP

TARGET AREA

♂
♀

AMMUNITION

ACTIVITY & SIGHTINGS

TYPES OF FLORA

ADDITIONAL NOTES

DATE	WEATHER CONDITIONS
TIME	
LOCATION	

HUNTING TYPE	TERRAIN LEVEL
CO-HUNTERS	EASY 1 2 3 4 5 HARD

GEAR/SETUP

TARGET AREA

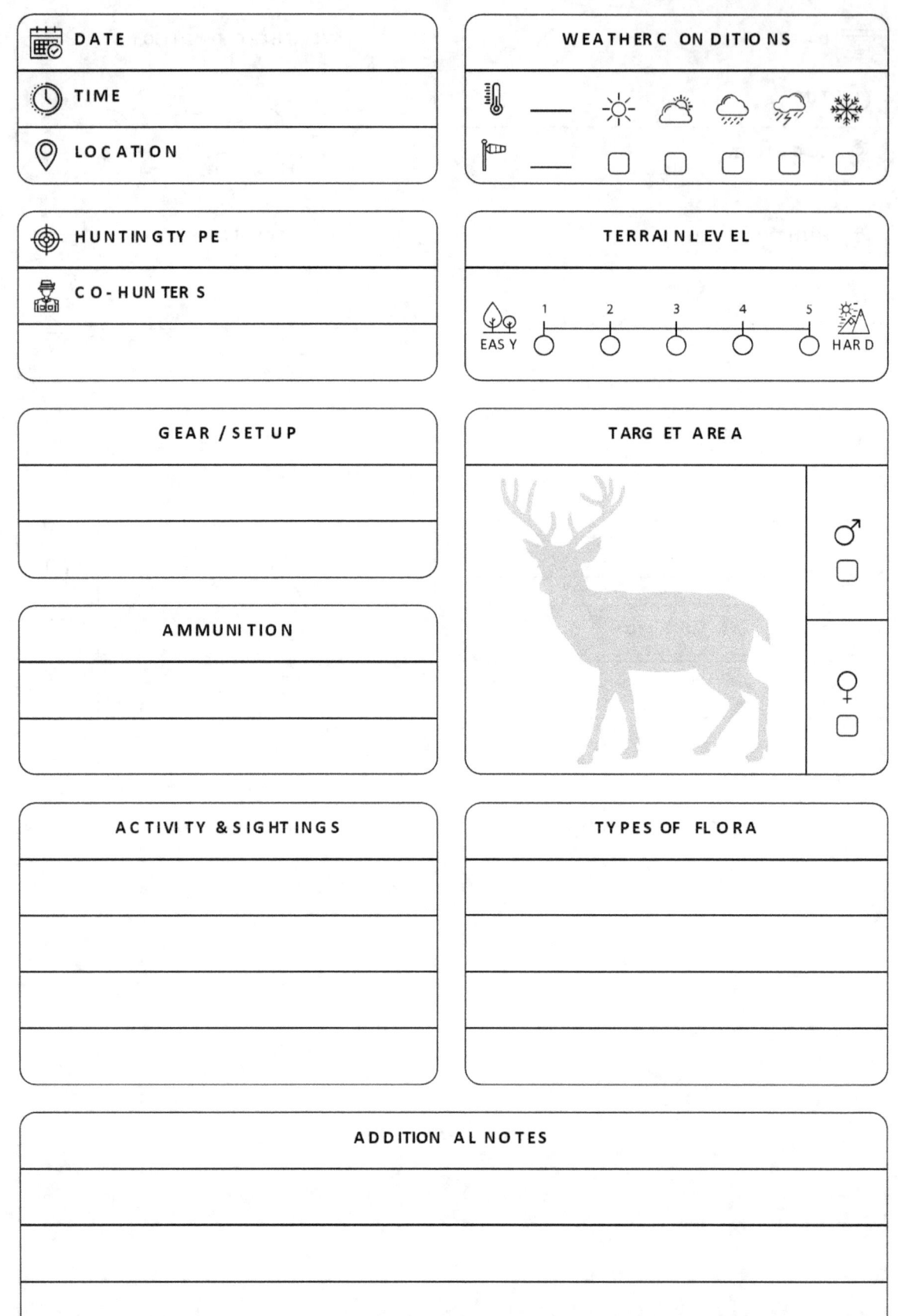

♂ ☐

♀ ☐

AMMUNITION

ACTIVITY & SIGHTINGS

TYPES OF FLORA

ADDITIONAL NOTES

DATE	WEATHER CONDITIONS
TIME	☀ ⛅ 🌧 ⛈ ❄
LOCATION	☐ ☐ ☐ ☐ ☐

HUNTING TYPE	TERRAIN LEVEL
CO-HUNTERS	EASY 1 2 3 4 5 HARD

GEAR / SETUP

TARGET AREA

♂ ☐

♀ ☐

AMMUNITION

ACTIVITY & SIGHTINGS

TYPES OF FLORA

ADDITIONAL NOTES

DATE	WEATHER CONDITIONS
TIME	☀️ ⛅ 🌧️ ⛈️ ❄️
LOCATION	☐ ☐ ☐ ☐ ☐

HUNTING TYPE

CO-HUNTERS

TERRAIN LEVEL

EASY 1 — 2 — 3 — 4 — 5 HARD

GEAR / SETUP

TARGET AREA

♂ ☐

♀ ☐

AMMUNITION

ACTIVITY & SIGHTINGS

TYPES OF FLORA

ADDITIONAL NOTES

DATE	WEATHER CONDITIONS
TIME	
LOCATION	

HUNTING TYPE	TERRAIN LEVEL
CO-HUNTERS	EASY 1 2 3 4 5 HARD

GEAR / SETUP

TARGET AREA

♂
♀

AMMUNITION

ACTIVITY & SIGHTINGS

TYPES OF FLORA

ADDITIONAL NOTES

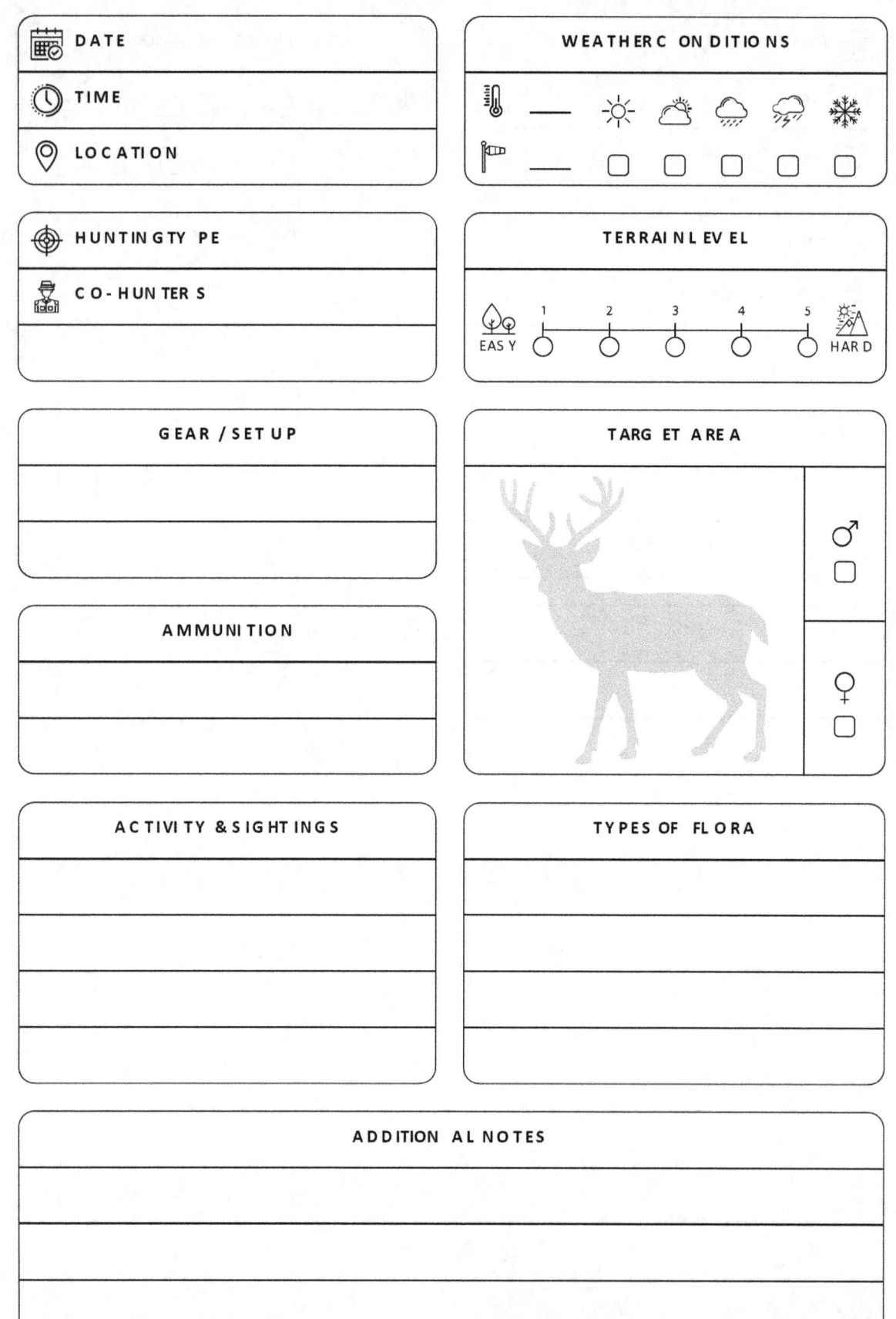

DATE	WEATHER CONDITIONS
TIME	☀️ ⛅ 🌧️ ⛈️ ❄️
LOCATION	☐ ☐ ☐ ☐ ☐

HUNTING TYPE	TERRAIN LEVEL
CO-HUNTERS	EASY 1 — 2 — 3 — 4 — 5 HARD

GEAR / SETUP

TARGET AREA

♂ ☐

♀ ☐

AMMUNITION

ACTIVITY & SIGHTINGS

TYPES OF FLORA

ADDITIONAL NOTES

DATE	WEATHER CONDITIONS

| TIME | |
| LOCATION | |

HUNTING TYPE	TERRAIN LEVEL
CO-HUNTERS	EASY 1 2 3 4 5 HARD

GEAR / SETUP	TARGET AREA

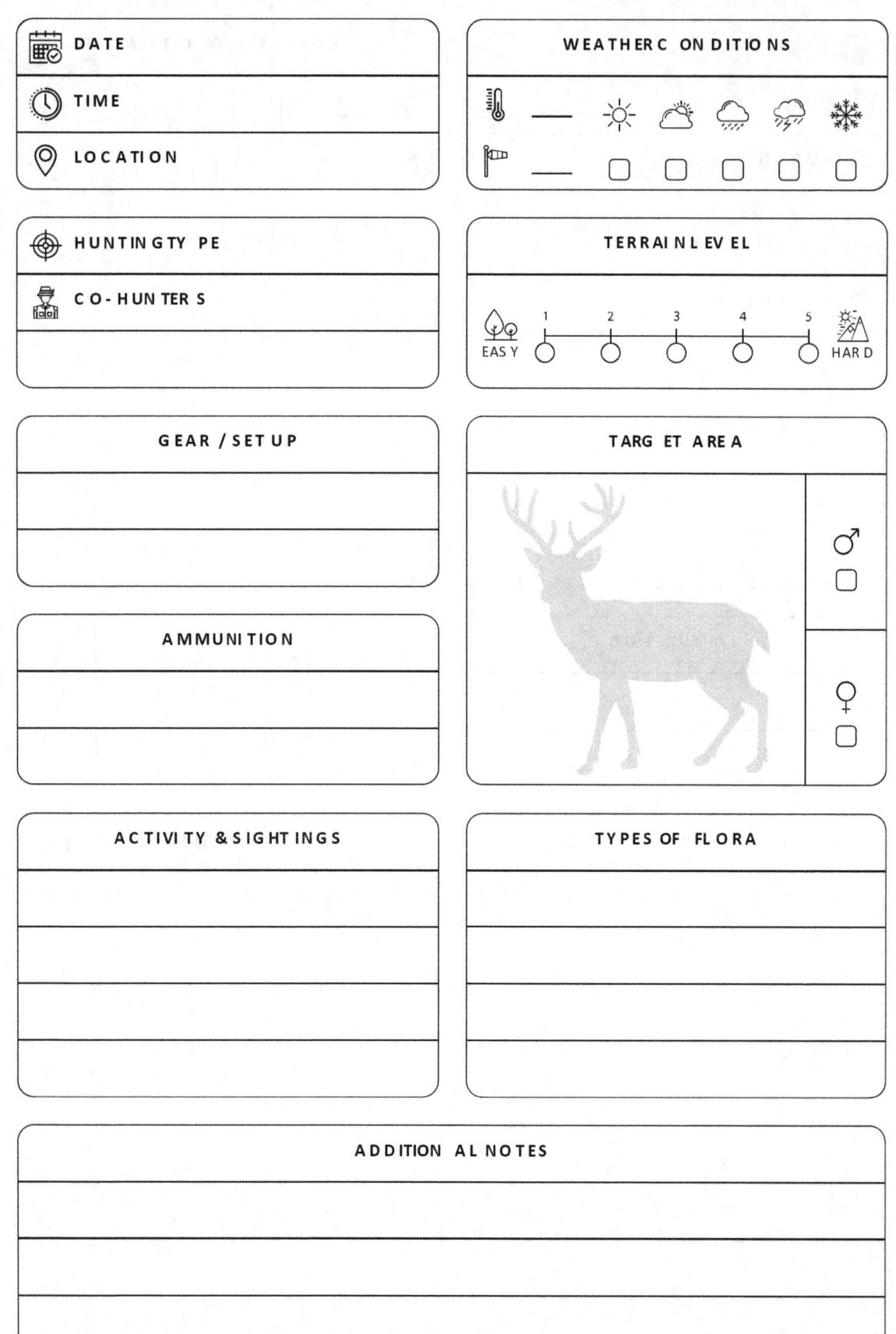

| AMMUNITION | |

ACTIVITY & SIGHTINGS	TYPES OF FLORA

ADDITIONAL NOTES

DATE	WEATHER CONDITIONS
TIME	
LOCATION	

HUNTING TYPE	TERRAIN LEVEL
CO-HUNTERS	EASY 1 2 3 4 5 HARD

GEAR / SETUP

TARGET AREA

♂ ☐

♀ ☐

AMMUNITION

ACTIVITY & SIGHTINGS

TYPES OF FLORA

ADDITIONAL NOTES

DATE

TIME

LOCATION

HUNTING TYPE

CO-HUNTERS

GEAR / SETUP

AMMUNITION

ACTIVITY & SIGHTINGS

WEATHER CONDITIONS

TERRAIN LEVEL

1   2   3   4   5

EASY — HARD

TARGET AREA

♂

♀

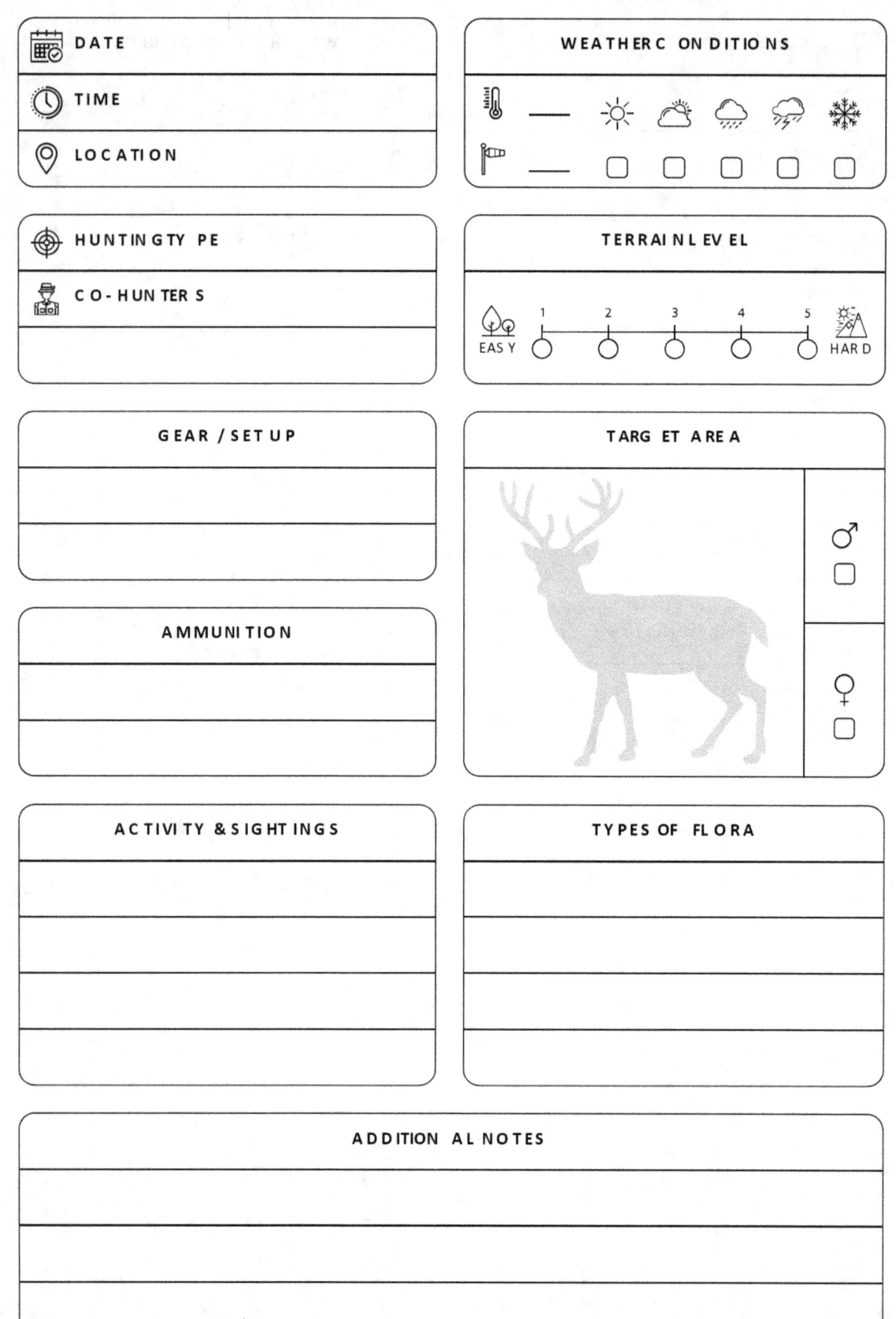

TYPES OF FLORA

ADDITIONAL NOTES

DATE	WEATHER CONDITIONS
TIME	
LOCATION	

HUNTING TYPE	TERRAIN LEVEL
CO-HUNTERS	EASY 1 2 3 4 5 HARD

GEAR / SETUP	TARGET AREA
AMMUNITION	♂ / ♀

ACTIVITY & SIGHTINGS	TYPES OF FLORA

ADDITIONAL NOTES

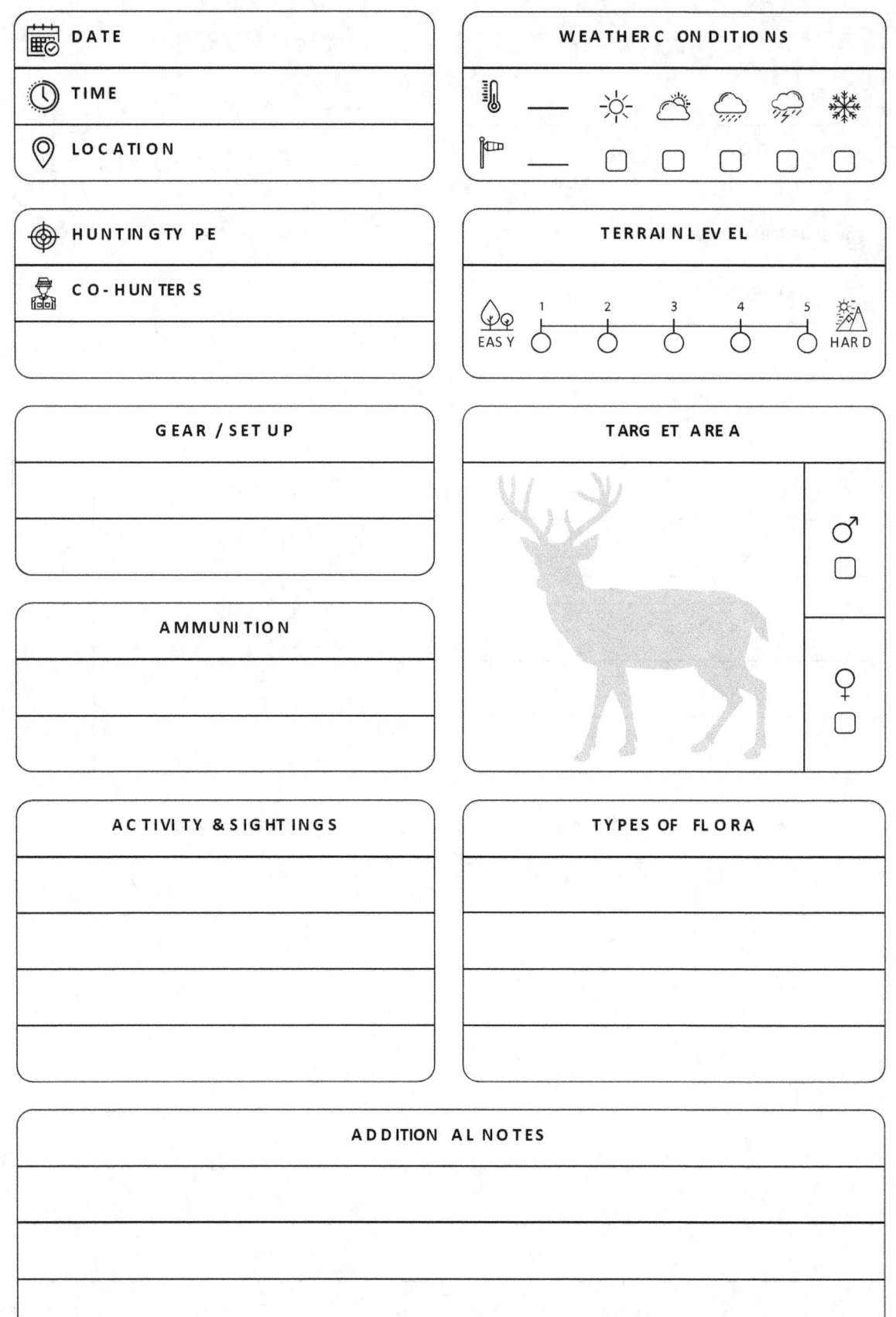

DATE	WEATHER CONDITIONS
TIME	☀️ ⛅ 🌧️ ⛈️ ❄️
LOCATION	☐ ☐ ☐ ☐ ☐

HUNTING TYPE	TERRAIN LEVEL
CO-HUNTERS	EASY 1 2 3 4 5 HARD

GEAR / SETUP

TARGET AREA

♂ ☐

♀ ☐

AMMUNITION

ACTIVITY & SIGHTINGS

TYPES OF FLORA

ADDITIONAL NOTES

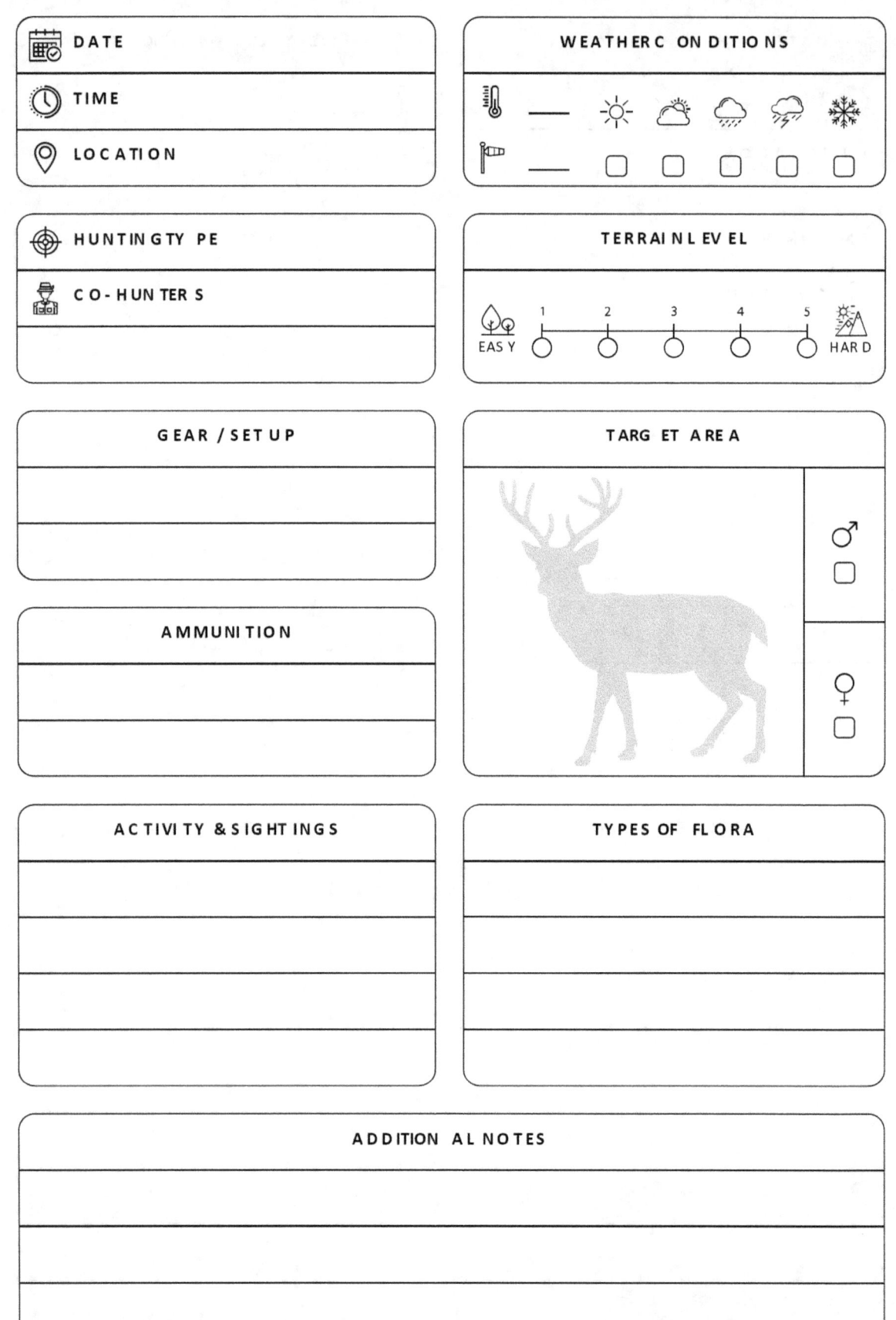

DATE

TIME

LOCATION

WEATHER CONDITIONS

HUNTING TYPE

CO-HUNTERS

TERRAIN LEVEL

EASY 1 2 3 4 5 HARD

GEAR / SETUP

TARGET AREA

♂

♀

AMMUNITION

ACTIVITY & SIGHTINGS

TYPES OF FLORA

ADDITIONAL NOTES

DATE
TIME
LOCATION

HUNTING TYPE
CO-HUNTERS

WEATHER CONDITIONS

🌡 ____   ☀ ⛅ 🌧 ⛈ ❄
🚩 ____   ☐ ☐ ☐ ☐ ☐

TERRAIN LEVEL

EASY 1 — 2 — 3 — 4 — 5 HARD

GEAR / SETUP

AMMUNITION

TARGET AREA

♂ ☐

♀ ☐

ACTIVITY & SIGHTINGS

TYPES OF FLORA

ADDITIONAL NOTES

DATE	WEATHER CONDITIONS
TIME	
LOCATION	

HUNTING TYPE	TERRAIN LEVEL
CO-HUNTERS	EASY 1 2 3 4 5 HARD

GEAR / SETUP	TARGET AREA
AMMUNITION	♂ ♀

ACTIVITY & SIGHTINGS	TYPES OF FLORA

ADDITIONAL NOTES

DATE

TIME

LOCATION

WEATHER CONDITIONS

HUNTING TYPE

CO-HUNTERS

TERRAIN LEVEL

EASY 1 2 3 4 5 HARD

GEAR / SETUP

TARGET AREA

♂

♀

AMMUNITION

ACTIVITY & SIGHTINGS

TYPES OF FLORA

ADDITIONAL NOTES

DATE	WEATHER CONDITIONS
TIME	
LOCATION	

HUNTING TYPE
CO-HUNTERS

TERRAIN LEVEL

EASY 1 2 3 4 5 HARD

GEAR / SETUP	TARGET AREA

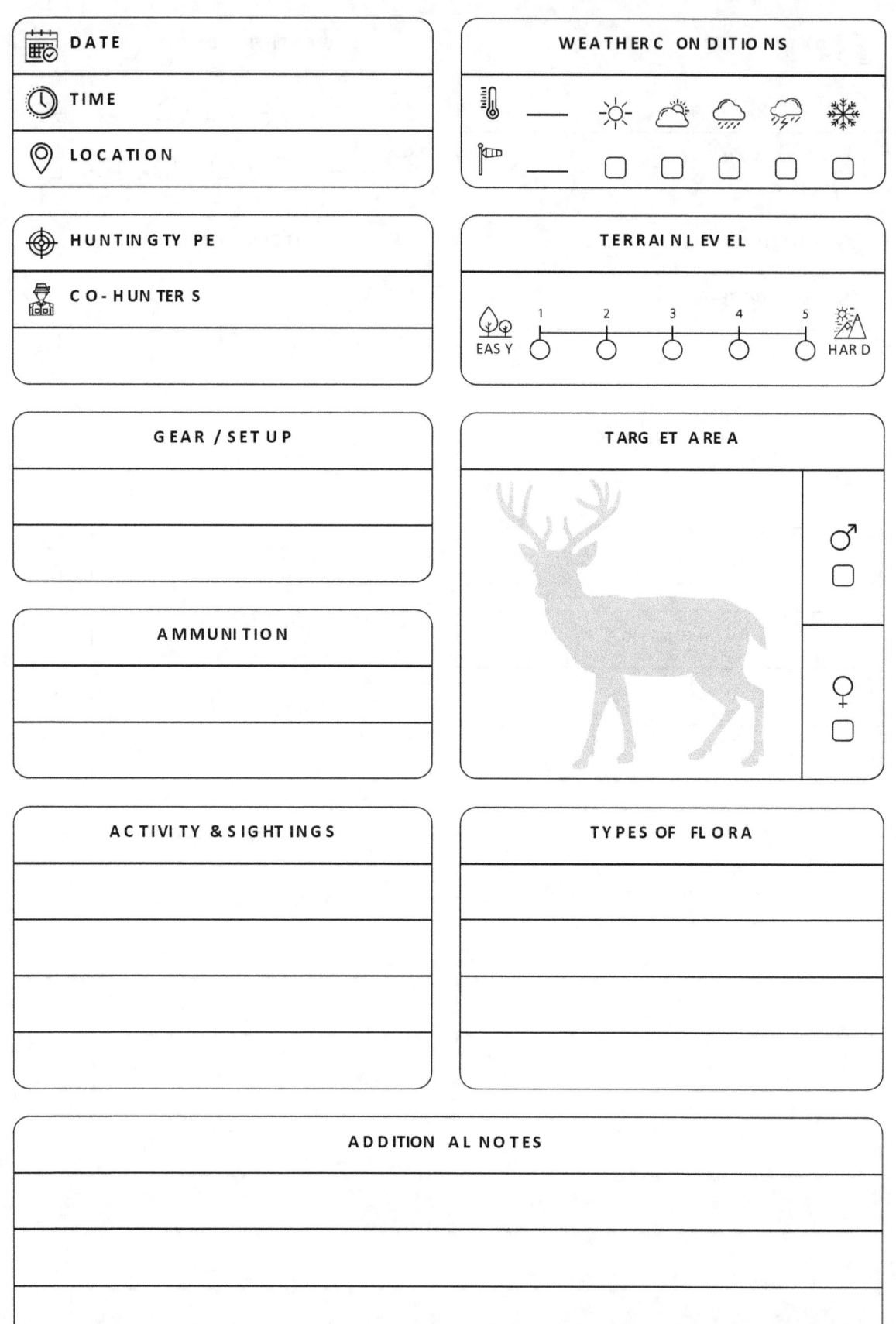

♂ ☐

♀ ☐

AMMUNITION

ACTIVITY & SIGHTINGS	TYPES OF FLORA

ADDITIONAL NOTES

📅 **DATE**	**WEATHER CONDITIONS**
🕐 **TIME**	🌡 ___ ☀ ⛅ 🌧 ⛈ ❄
📍 **LOCATION**	🚩 ___ ☐ ☐ ☐ ☐ ☐

HUNTING TYPE

CO-HUNTERS

TERRAIN LEVEL

EASY 1 2 3 4 5 HARD

GEAR / SETUP

TARGET AREA

♂ ☐

♀ ☐

AMMUNITION

ACTIVITY & SIGHTINGS

TYPES OF FLORA

ADDITIONAL NOTES

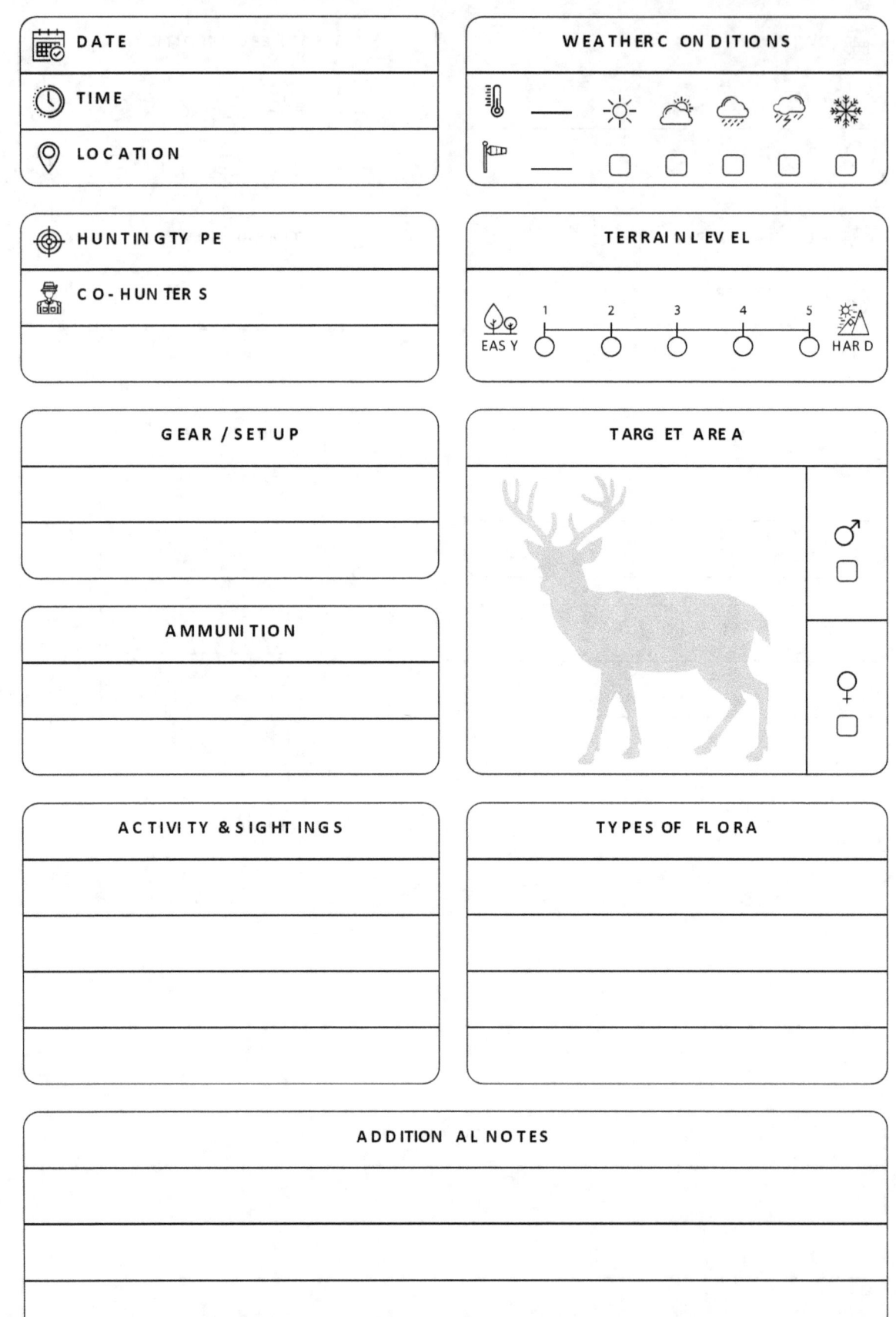

DATE	WEATHER CONDITIONS
TIME	
LOCATION	

HUNTING TYPE	TERRAIN LEVEL
CO-HUNTERS	EASY 1 2 3 4 5 HARD

GEAR / SETUP	TARGET AREA
	♂
AMMUNITION	♀

ACTIVITY & SIGHTINGS	TYPES OF FLORA

ADDITIONAL NOTES

DATE	WEATHER CONDITIONS
TIME	
LOCATION	

HUNTING TYPE	TERRAIN LEVEL
CO-HUNTERS	EASY 1 2 3 4 5 HARD

GEAR / SETUP	TARGET AREA
AMMUNITION	♂ ☐ ♀ ☐

ACTIVITY & SIGHTINGS	TYPES OF FLORA

ADDITIONAL NOTES

DATE	WEATHER CONDITIONS
TIME	☀ ⛅ 🌧 ⛈ ❄
LOCATION	☐ ☐ ☐ ☐ ☐

HUNTING TYPE	TERRAIN LEVEL
CO-HUNTERS	EASY 1 2 3 4 5 HARD

GEAR / SETUP

TARGET AREA

♂ ☐

♀ ☐

AMMUNITION

ACTIVITY & SIGHTINGS

TYPES OF FLORA

ADDITIONAL NOTES

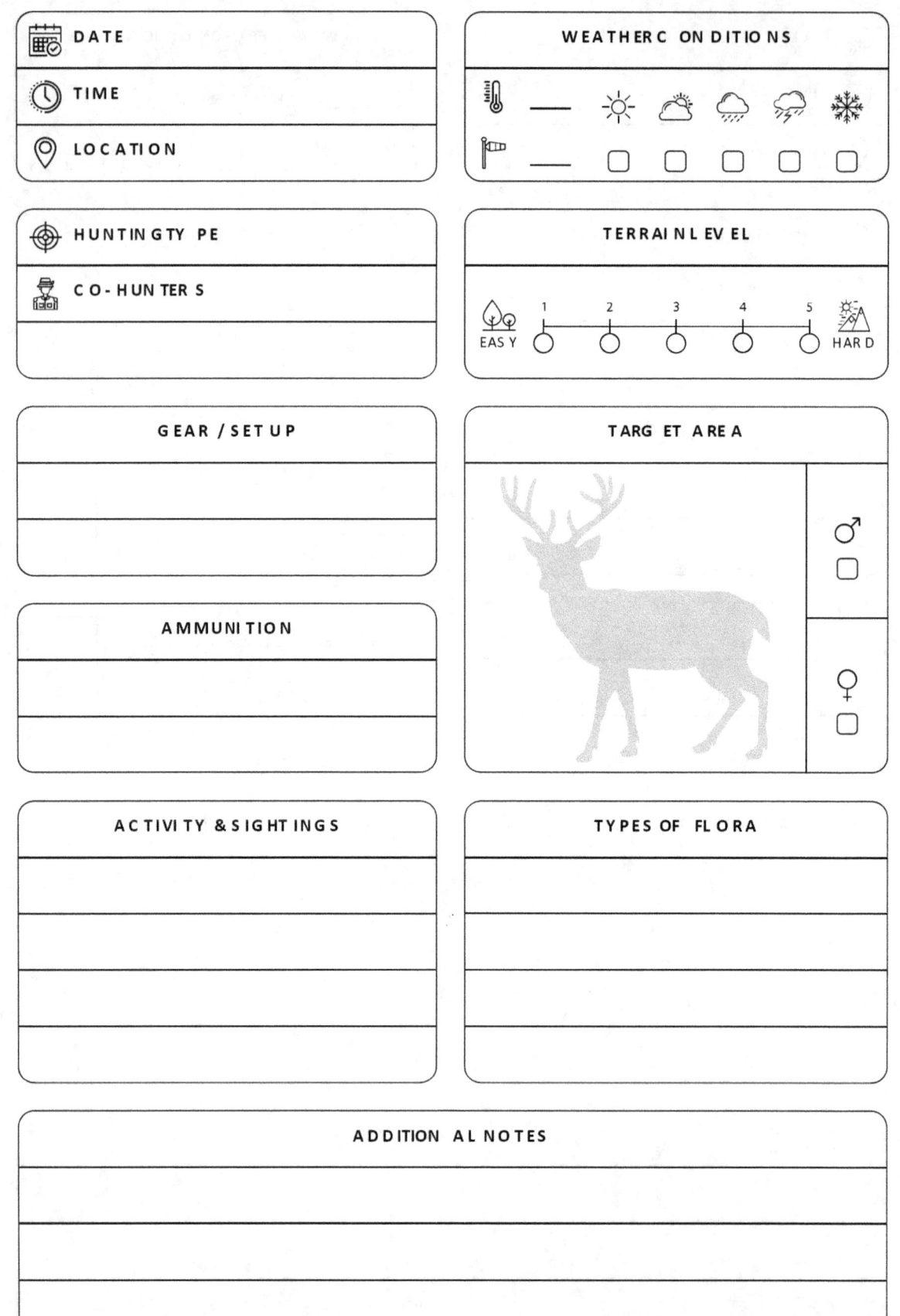

DATE	WEATHER CONDITIONS
TIME	
LOCATION	

HUNTING TYPE	TERRAIN LEVEL
CO-HUNTERS	EASY 1 2 3 4 5 HARD

GEAR / SETUP	TARGET AREA
AMMUNITION	♂ / ♀

ACTIVITY & SIGHTINGS	TYPES OF FLORA

ADDITIONAL NOTES

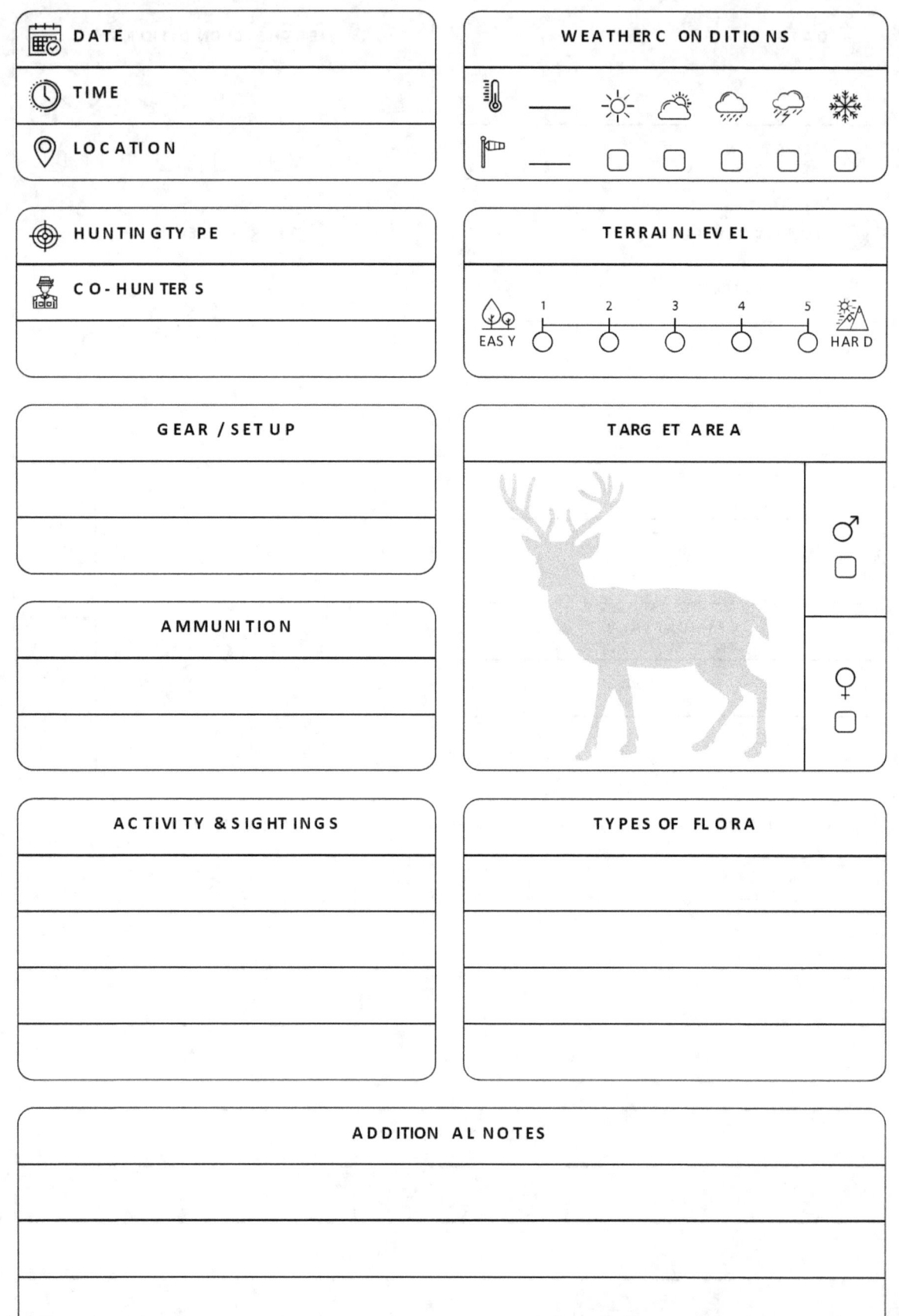

DATE	WEATHER CONDITIONS
TIME	☀️ ⛅ 🌧️ ⛈️ ❄️
LOCATION	☐ ☐ ☐ ☐ ☐

HUNTING TYPE	TERRAIN LEVEL
CO-HUNTERS	EASY 1 — 2 — 3 — 4 — 5 HARD ○ ○ ○ ○ ○

GEAR / SETUP

TARGET AREA

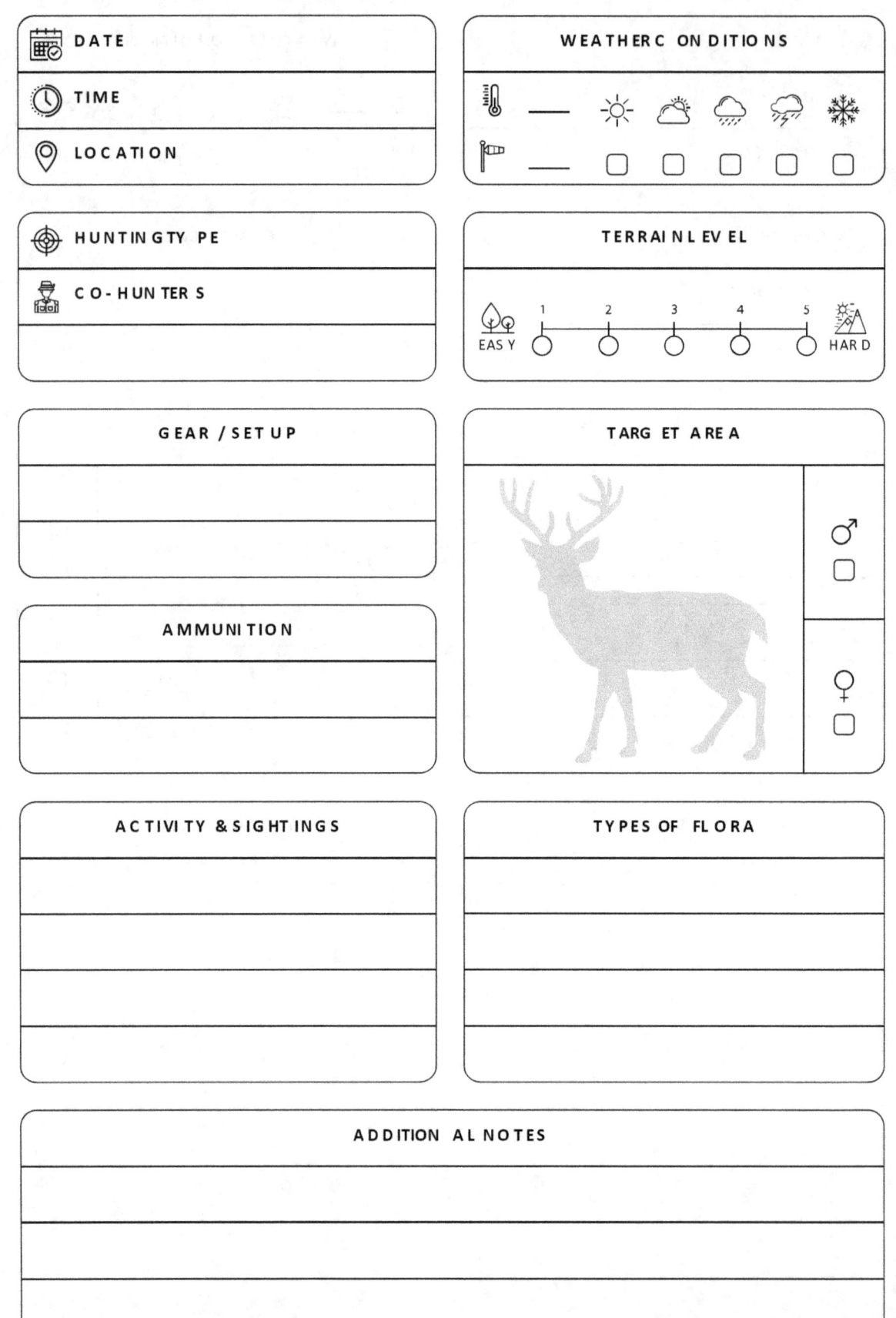

♂ ☐

♀ ☐

AMMUNITION

ACTIVITY & SIGHTINGS

TYPES OF FLORA

ADDITIONAL NOTES

DATE	WEATHER CONDITIONS
TIME	
LOCATION	

HUNTING TYPE	TERRAIN LEVEL
CO-HUNTERS	EASY 1 2 3 4 5 HARD

GEAR / SETUP	TARGET AREA
AMMUNITION	♂ / ♀

ACTIVITY & SIGHTINGS	TYPES OF FLORA

ADDITIONAL NOTES

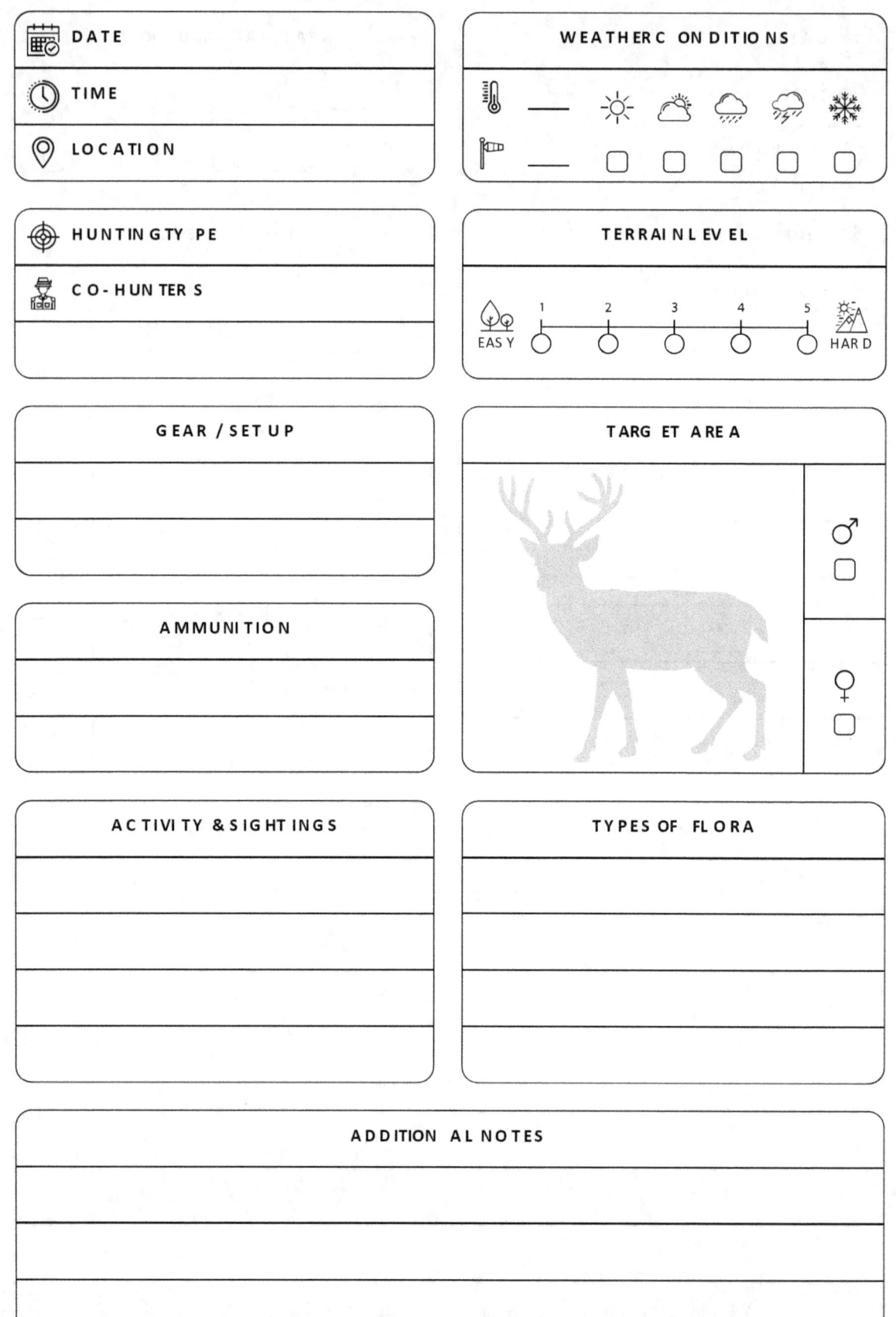

DATE	WEATHER CONDITIONS
TIME	☀ ⛅ 🌧 ⛈ ❄
LOCATION	☐ ☐ ☐ ☐ ☐

HUNTING TYPE	TERRAIN LEVEL
CO-HUNTERS	1 2 3 4 5
	EASY ○ ○ ○ ○ ○ HARD

GEAR / SETUP

TARGET AREA

♂ ☐

♀ ☐

AMMUNITION

ACTIVITY & SIGHTINGS

TYPES OF FLORA

ADDITIONAL NOTES

DATE	WEATHER CONDITIONS
TIME	
LOCATION	

HUNTING TYPE	TERRAIN LEVEL
CO-HUNTERS	EASY 1 2 3 4 5 HARD

GEAR / SETUP	TARGET AREA
AMMUNITION	♂ / ♀

ACTIVITY & SIGHTINGS	TYPES OF FLORA

ADDITIONAL NOTES

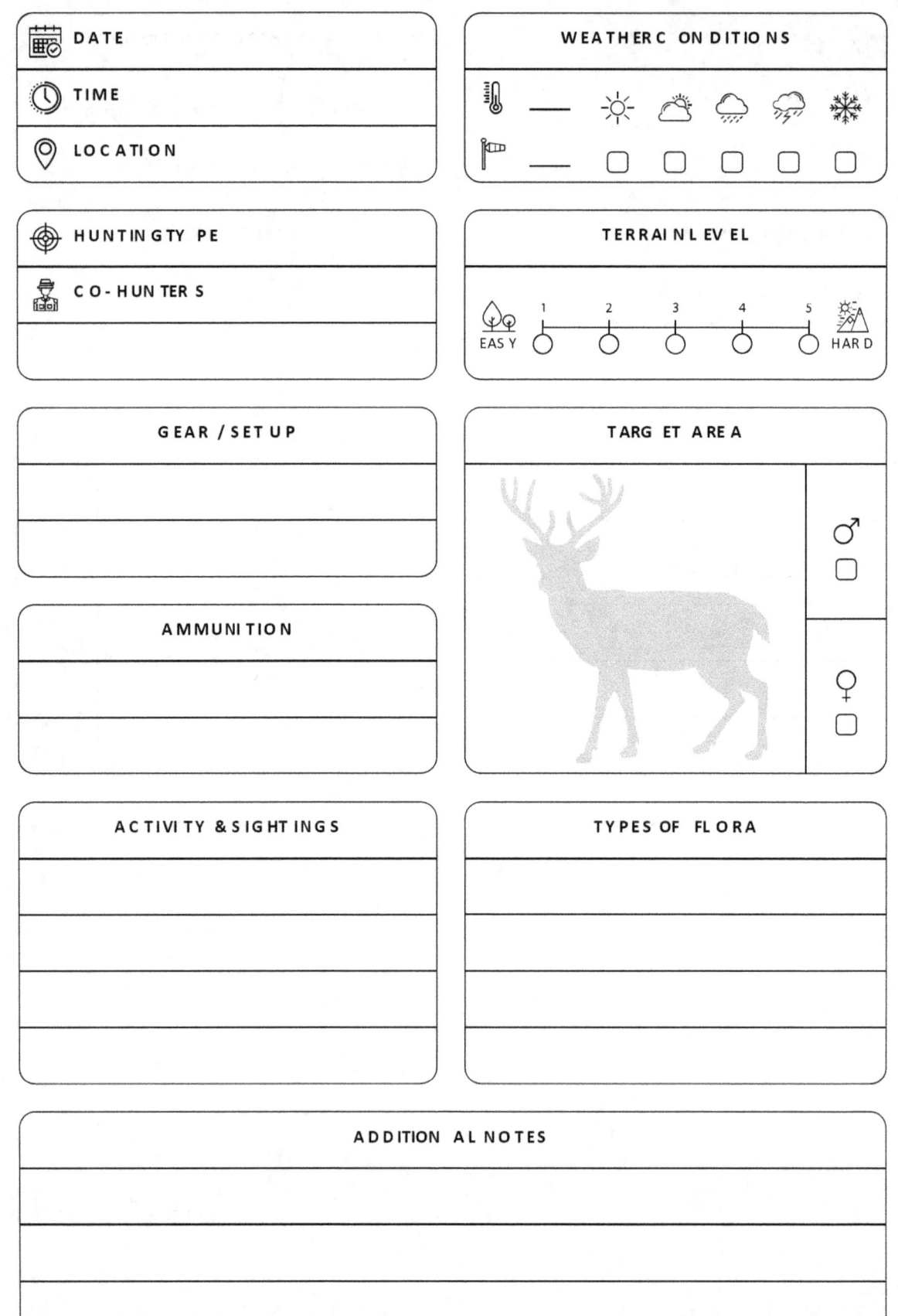

DATE	**WEATHER CONDITIONS**
TIME	☀️ ⛅ 🌧️ ⛈️ ❄️
LOCATION	🌬️ ☐ ☐ ☐ ☐ ☐

HUNTING TYPE

CO-HUNTERS

TERRAIN LEVEL

EASY 1 — 2 — 3 — 4 — 5 HARD

GEAR / SETUP

TARGET AREA

♂ ☐

♀ ☐

AMMUNITION

ACTIVITY & SIGHTINGS

TYPES OF FLORA

ADDITIONAL NOTES

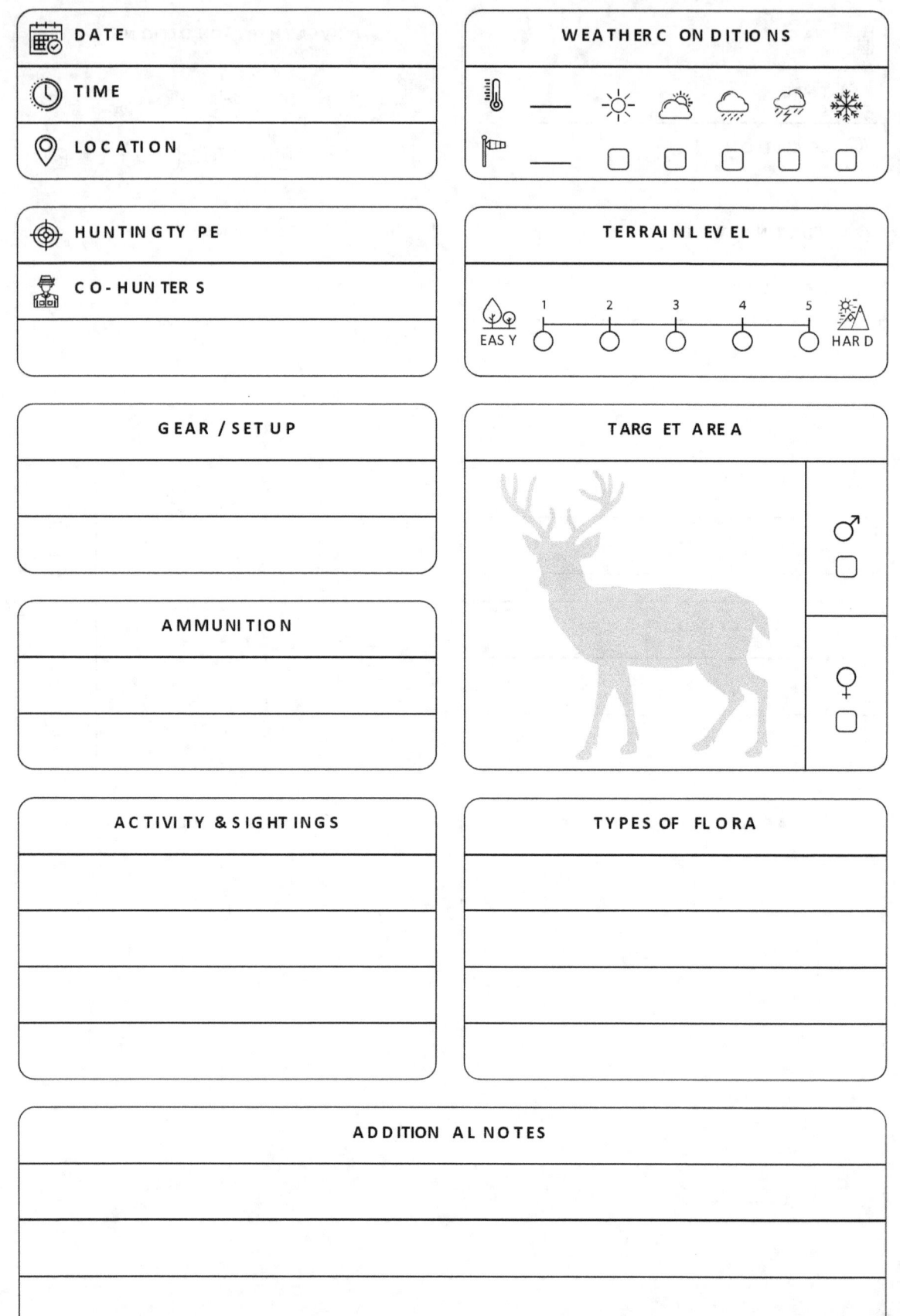

DATE	WEATHER CONDITIONS
TIME	☀️ ⛅ 🌧️ ⛈️ ❄️
LOCATION	☐ ☐ ☐ ☐ ☐

HUNTING TYPE

CO-HUNTERS

TERRAIN LEVEL

EASY 1 — 2 — 3 — 4 — 5 HARD

GEAR / SETUP

TARGET AREA

♂ ☐

♀ ☐

AMMUNITION

ACTIVITY & SIGHTINGS

TYPES OF FLORA

ADDITIONAL NOTES

DATE	
TIME	
LOCATION	

HUNTING TYPE	
CO-HUNTERS	

WEATHER CONDITIONS

🌡 _____ ☀ ⛅ 🌧 ⛈ ❄
🚩 _____ ☐ ☐ ☐ ☐ ☐

TERRAIN LEVEL

EASY 1 — 2 — 3 — 4 — 5 HARD

GEAR / SETUP

AMMUNITION

TARGET AREA

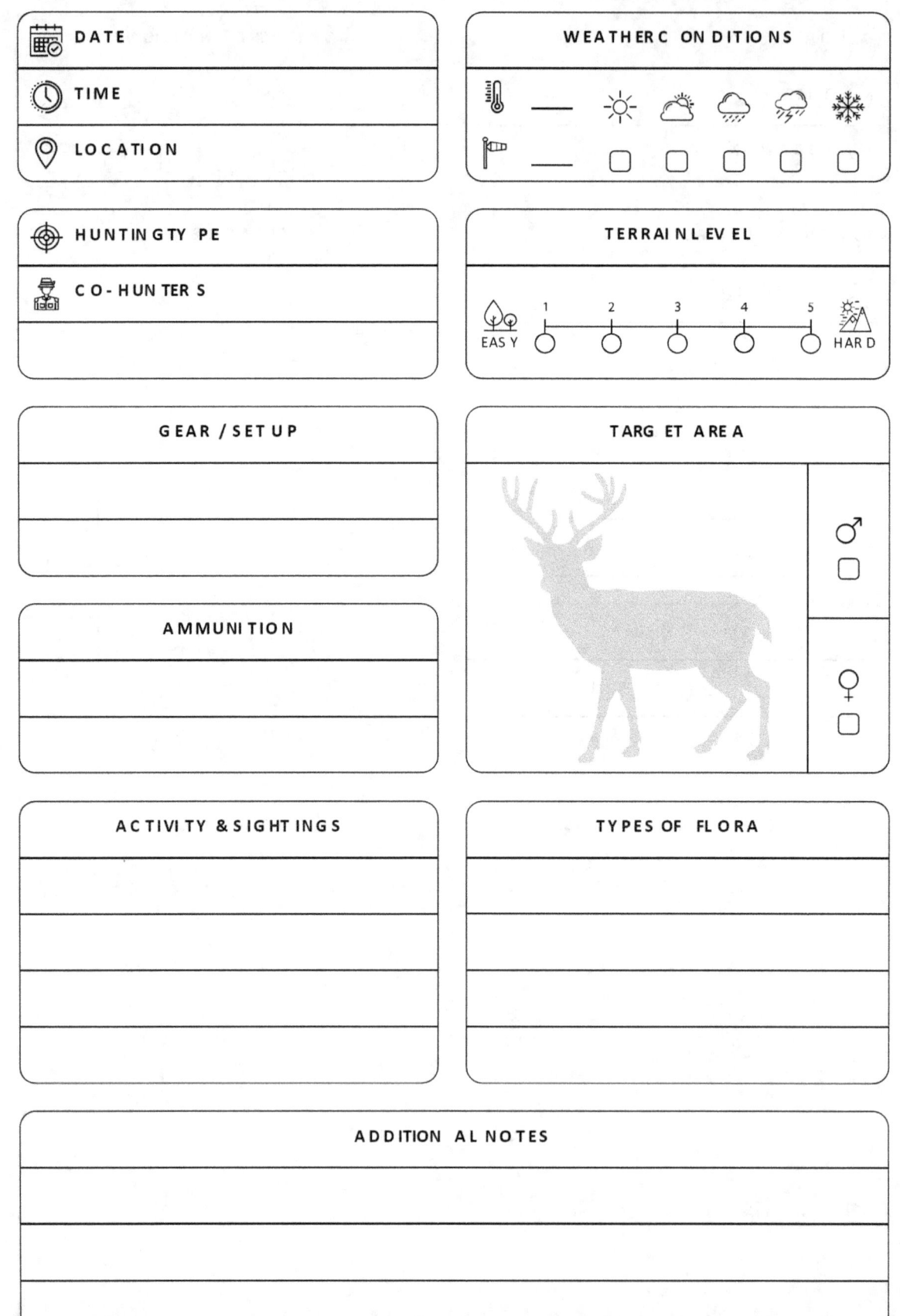

♂ ☐

♀ ☐

ACTIVITY & SIGHTINGS

TYPES OF FLORA

ADDITIONAL NOTES

DATE
TIME
LOCATION

WEATHER CONDITIONS

🌡 ____ ☀ ⛅ 🌧 ⛈ ❄
🚩 ____ ☐ ☐ ☐ ☐ ☐

HUNTING TYPE
CO-HUNTERS

TERRAIN LEVEL

EASY 1—2—3—4—5 HARD

GEAR / SETUP

AMMUNITION

TARGET AREA

♂ ☐

♀ ☐

ACTIVITY & SIGHTINGS

TYPES OF FLORA

ADDITIONAL NOTES

DATE	WEATHER CONDITIONS
TIME	☀ ⛅ 🌧 ⛈ ❄
LOCATION	☐ ☐ ☐ ☐ ☐

HUNTING TYPE	TERRAIN LEVEL
CO-HUNTERS	EASY 1 2 3 4 5 HARD

GEAR / SETUP

TARGET AREA

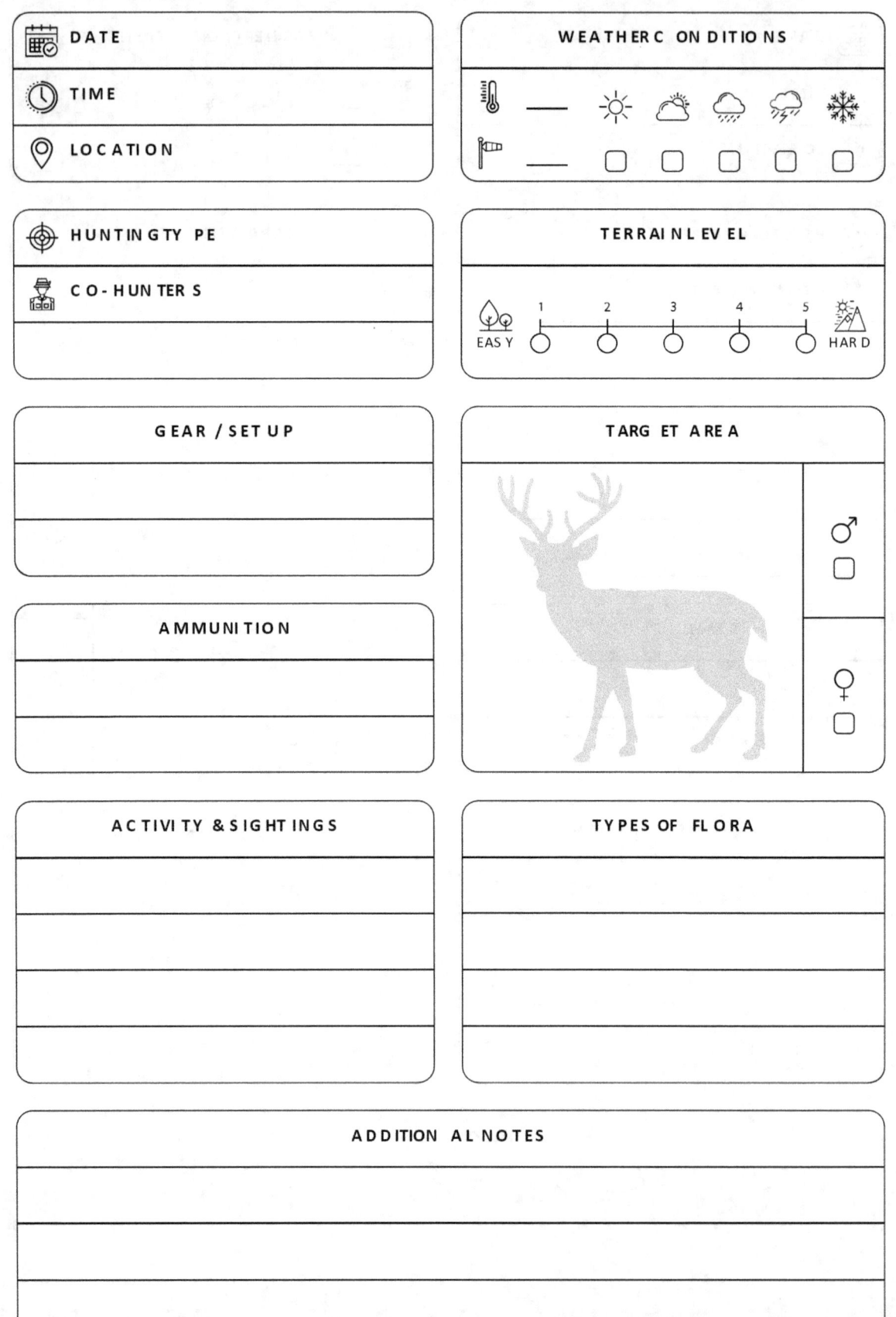

♂ ☐

♀ ☐

AMMUNITION

ACTIVITY & SIGHTINGS

TYPES OF FLORA

ADDITIONAL NOTES

DATE

TIME

LOCATION

HUNTING TYPE

CO-HUNTERS

WEATHER CONDITIONS

TERRAIN LEVEL

EASY 1 2 3 4 5 HARD

GEAR / SETUP

AMMUNITION

TARGET AREA

♂

♀

ACTIVITY & SIGHTINGS

TYPES OF FLORA

ADDITIONAL NOTES

DATE	WEATHER CONDITIONS
TIME	
LOCATION	

HUNTING TYPE	TERRAIN LEVEL
CO-HUNTERS	EASY 1 2 3 4 5 HARD

GEAR / SETUP

TARGET AREA

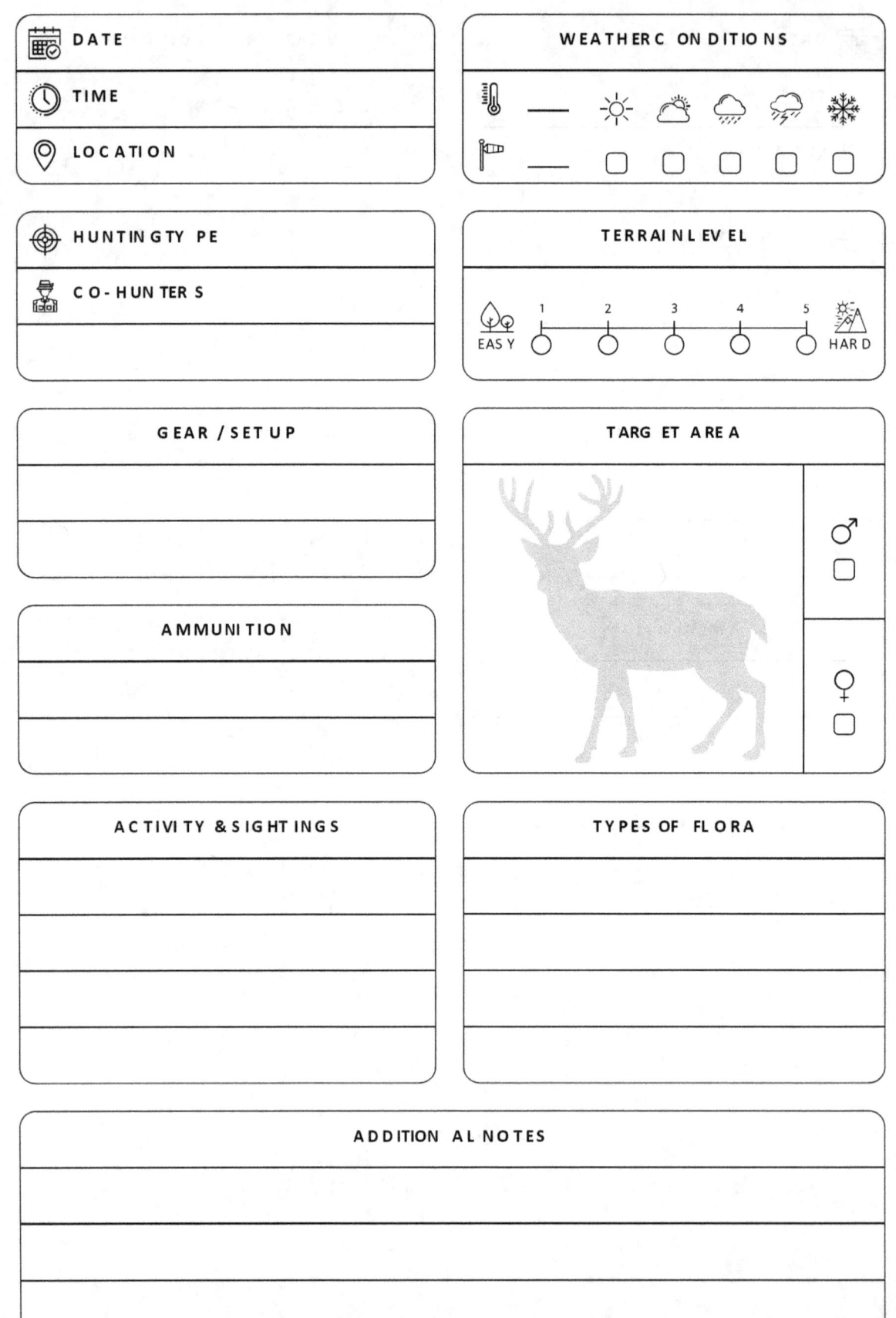

♂ ☐

♀ ☐

AMMUNITION

ACTIVITY & SIGHTINGS

TYPES OF FLORA

ADDITIONAL NOTES

DATE	WEATHER CONDITIONS
TIME	
LOCATION	

HUNTING TYPE	TERRAIN LEVEL
CO-HUNTERS	EASY 1 2 3 4 5 HARD

GEAR / SETUP	TARGET AREA
AMMUNITION	♂ ♀

ACTIVITY & SIGHTINGS	TYPES OF FLORA

ADDITIONAL NOTES

DATE	WEATHER CONDITIONS
TIME	
LOCATION	

HUNTING TYPE	TERRAIN LEVEL
CO-HUNTERS	EASY 1 2 3 4 5 HARD

GEAR / SETUP	TARGET AREA
AMMUNITION	♂ / ♀

ACTIVITY & SIGHTINGS	TYPES OF FLORA

ADDITIONAL NOTES

DATE	WEATHER CONDITIONS
TIME	
LOCATION	

- HUNTING TYPE
- CO-HUNTERS

TERRAIN LEVEL

EASY 1 2 3 4 5 HARD

GEAR / SETUP

AMMUNITION

TARGET AREA

♂ ☐

♀ ☐

ACTIVITY & SIGHTINGS

TYPES OF FLORA

ADDITIONAL NOTES

DATE	WEATHER CONDITIONS
TIME	☀️ ⛅ 🌧️ ⛈️ ❄️
LOCATION	

HUNTING TYPE	TERRAIN LEVEL
CO-HUNTERS	EASY 1 — 2 — 3 — 4 — 5 HARD

GEAR / SETUP

TARGET AREA

♂
♀

AMMUNITION

ACTIVITY & SIGHTINGS

TYPES OF FLORA

ADDITIONAL NOTES

DATE

TIME

LOCATION

WEATHER CONDITIONS

HUNTING TYPE

CO-HUNTERS

TERRAIN LEVEL

EASY 1 2 3 4 5 HARD

GEAR / SETUP

TARGET AREA

♂

♀

AMMUNITION

ACTIVITY & SIGHTINGS

TYPES OF FLORA

ADDITIONAL NOTES

DATE
TIME
LOCATION

WEATHER CONDITIONS

🌡 ____ ☀ ⛅ 🌧 ⛈ ❄
🚩 ____ ☐ ☐ ☐ ☐ ☐

HUNTING TYPE
CO-HUNTERS

TERRAIN LEVEL

EASY 1 — 2 — 3 — 4 — 5 HARD

GEAR / SETUP

TARGET AREA

♂ ☐

♀ ☐

AMMUNITION

ACTIVITY & SIGHTINGS

TYPES OF FLORA

ADDITIONAL NOTES

DATE	WEATHER CONDITIONS
TIME	☀ ⛅ 🌧 ⛈ ❄
LOCATION	☐ ☐ ☐ ☐ ☐

HUNTING TYPE
CO-HUNTERS

TERRAIN LEVEL
EASY 1 2 3 4 5 HARD

GEAR / SETUP

TARGET AREA
♂ ☐
♀ ☐

AMMUNITION

ACTIVITY & SIGHTINGS

TYPES OF FLORA

ADDITIONAL NOTES

DATE	WEATHER CONDITIONS
TIME	
LOCATION	

HUNTING TYPE	TERRAIN LEVEL
CO-HUNTERS	EASY 1 2 3 4 5 HARD

GEAR / SETUP	TARGET AREA
AMMUNITION	♂ ♀

ACTIVITY & SIGHTINGS	TYPES OF FLORA

ADDITIONAL NOTES

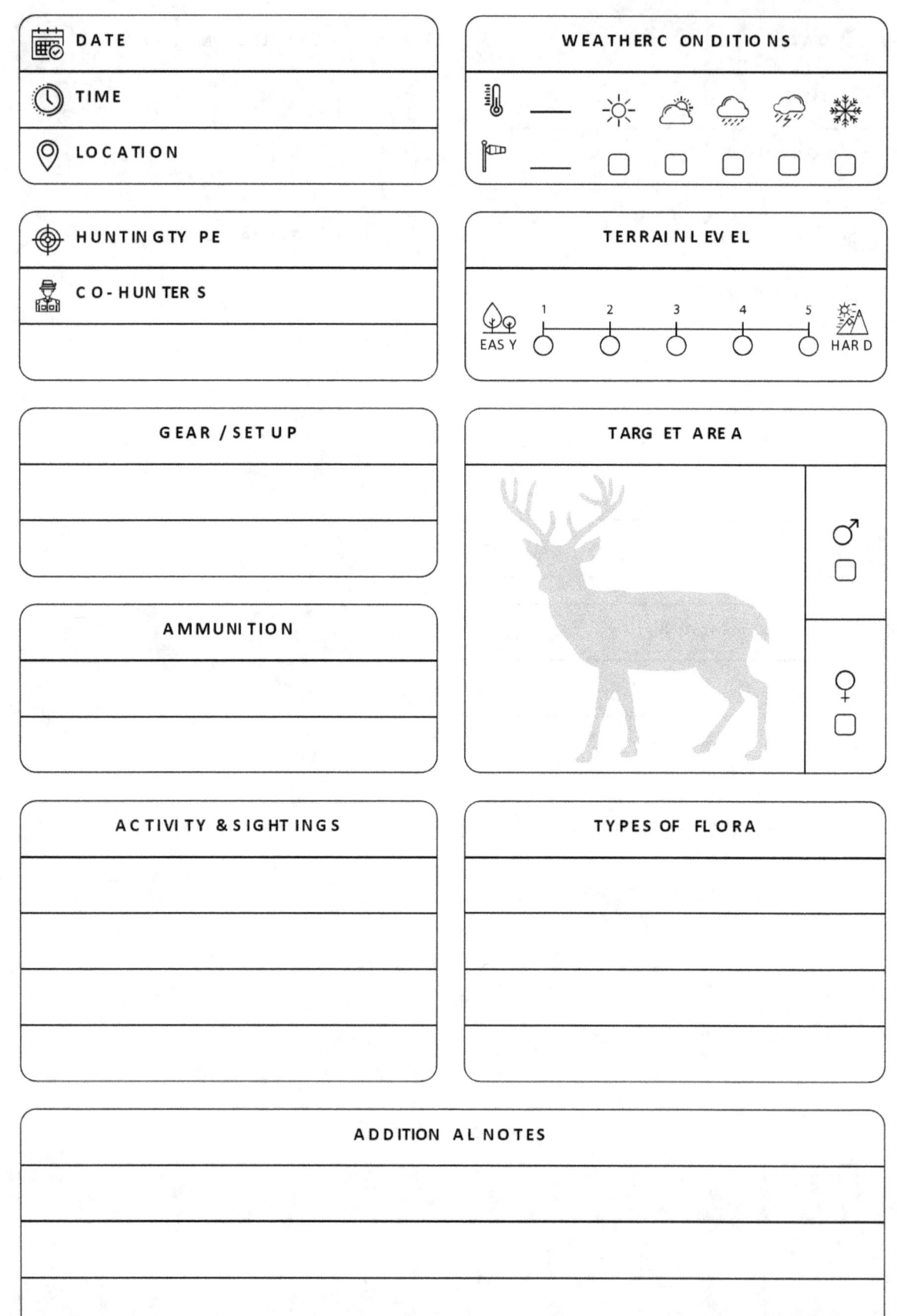

DATE	WEATHER CONDITIONS
TIME	
LOCATION	

HUNTING TYPE	TERRAIN LEVEL
CO-HUNTERS	EASY 1 2 3 4 5 HARD

GEAR / SETUP	TARGET AREA
	♂ ☐
AMMUNITION	♀ ☐

ACTIVITY & SIGHTINGS	TYPES OF FLORA

ADDITIONAL NOTES

DATE	WEATHER CONDITIONS
TIME	
LOCATION	

- HUNTING TYPE
- CO-HUNTERS

TERRAIN LEVEL

EASY 1 — 2 — 3 — 4 — 5 HARD

GEAR / SETUP

TARGET AREA

♂
♀

AMMUNITION

ACTIVITY & SIGHTINGS

TYPES OF FLORA

ADDITIONAL NOTES

📅 DATE	WEATHER CONDITIONS
🕐 TIME	🌡 ____ ☀️ ⛅ 🌧 ⛈ ❄️
📍 LOCATION	🚩 ____ ☐ ☐ ☐ ☐ ☐

HUNTING TYPE
CO-HUNTERS

TERRAIN LEVEL
EASY 1 2 3 4 5 HARD

GEAR / SETUP

TARGET AREA
♂ ☐
♀ ☐

AMMUNITION

ACTIVITY & SIGHTINGS

TYPES OF FLORA

ADDITIONAL NOTES

DATE	WEATHER CONDITIONS
TIME	
LOCATION	

HUNTING TYPE	TERRAIN LEVEL
CO-HUNTERS	EASY 1 2 3 4 5 HARD

GEAR / SETUP	TARGET AREA

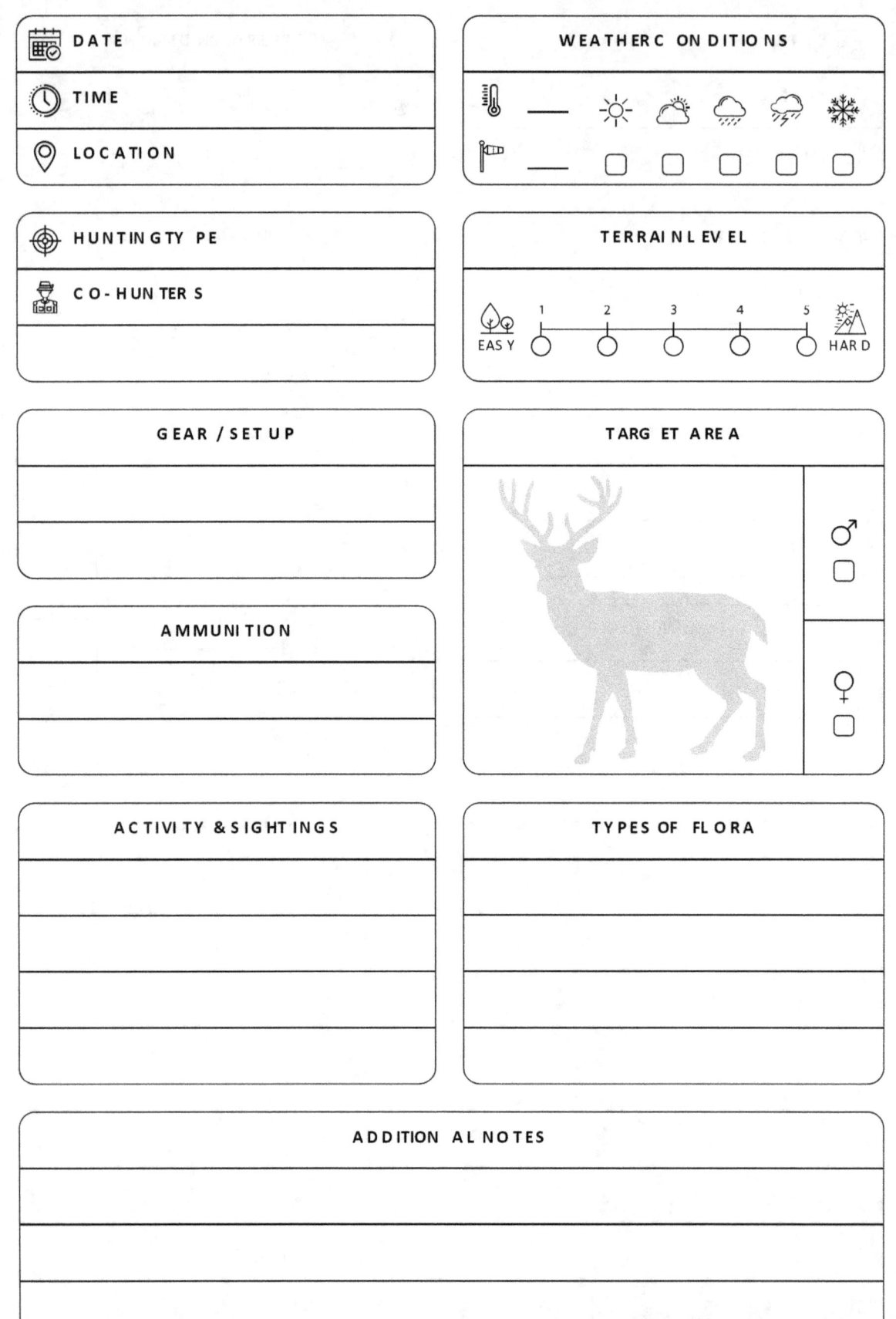

♂
♀

AMMUNITION

ACTIVITY & SIGHTINGS	TYPES OF FLORA

ADDITIONAL NOTES

DATE
TIME
LOCATION

HUNTING TYPE
CO-HUNTERS

WEATHER CONDITIONS

🌡 _____ ☀️ ⛅ 🌧 ⛈ ❄️
🪁 _____ ☐ ☐ ☐ ☐ ☐

TERRAIN LEVEL

EASY 1 2 3 4 5 HARD

GEAR / SETUP

AMMUNITION

TARGET AREA

♂ ☐

♀ ☐

ACTIVITY & SIGHTINGS

TYPES OF FLORA

ADDITIONAL NOTES

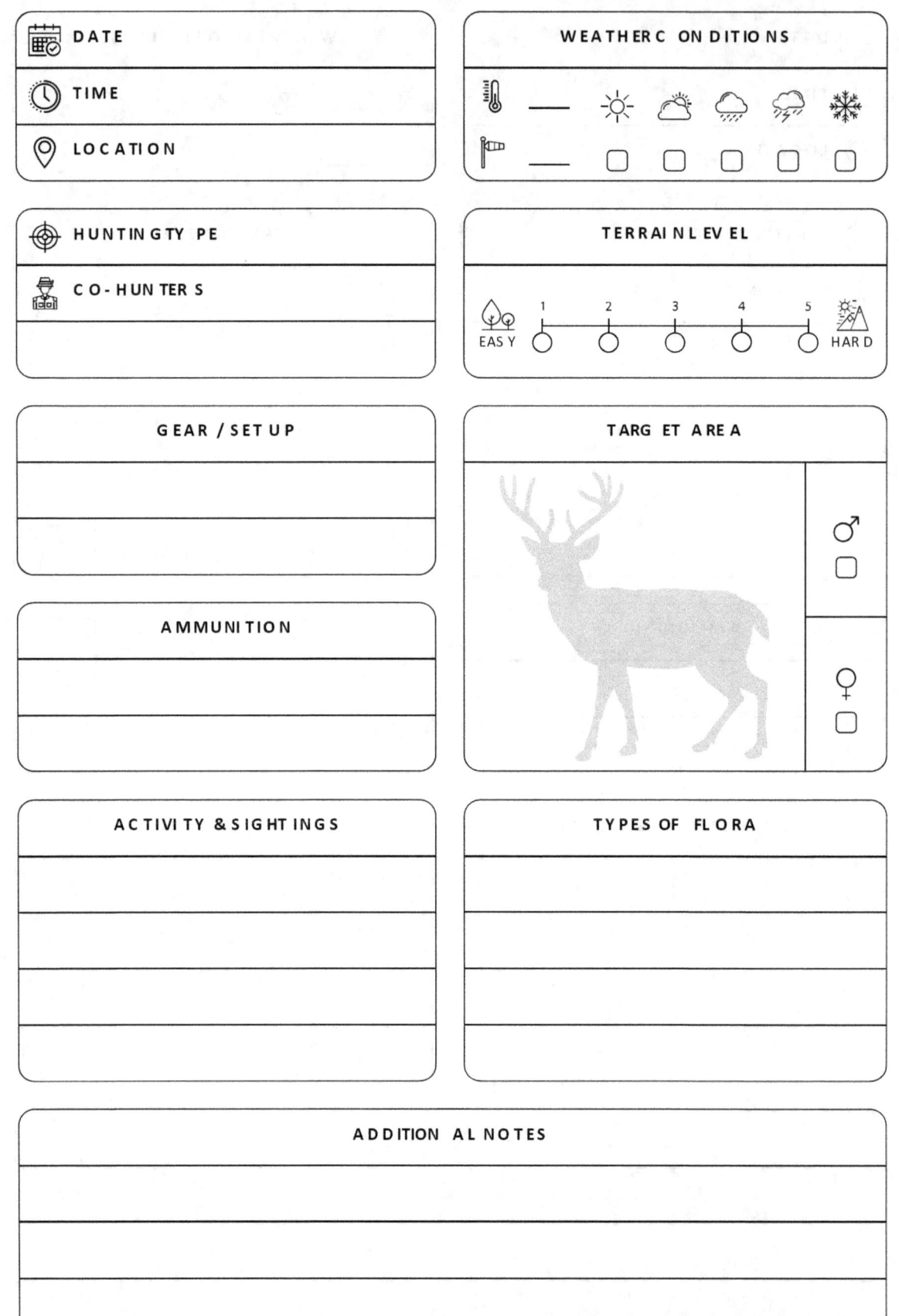

DATE	
TIME	
LOCATION	

WEATHER CONDITIONS

HUNTING TYPE
CO-HUNTERS

TERRAIN LEVEL
EASY 1 2 3 4 5 HARD

GEAR / SETUP

TARGET AREA
♂
♀

AMMUNITION

ACTIVITY & SIGHTINGS

TYPES OF FLORA

ADDITIONAL NOTES

DATE	WEATHER CONDITIONS
TIME	☀ ⛅ 🌧 ⛈ ❄
LOCATION	☐ ☐ ☐ ☐ ☐

HUNTING TYPE

CO-HUNTERS

TERRAIN LEVEL

EASY 1 2 3 4 5 HARD

GEAR / SETUP

TARGET AREA

♂ ☐

♀ ☐

AMMUNITION

ACTIVITY & SIGHTINGS

TYPES OF FLORA

ADDITIONAL NOTES

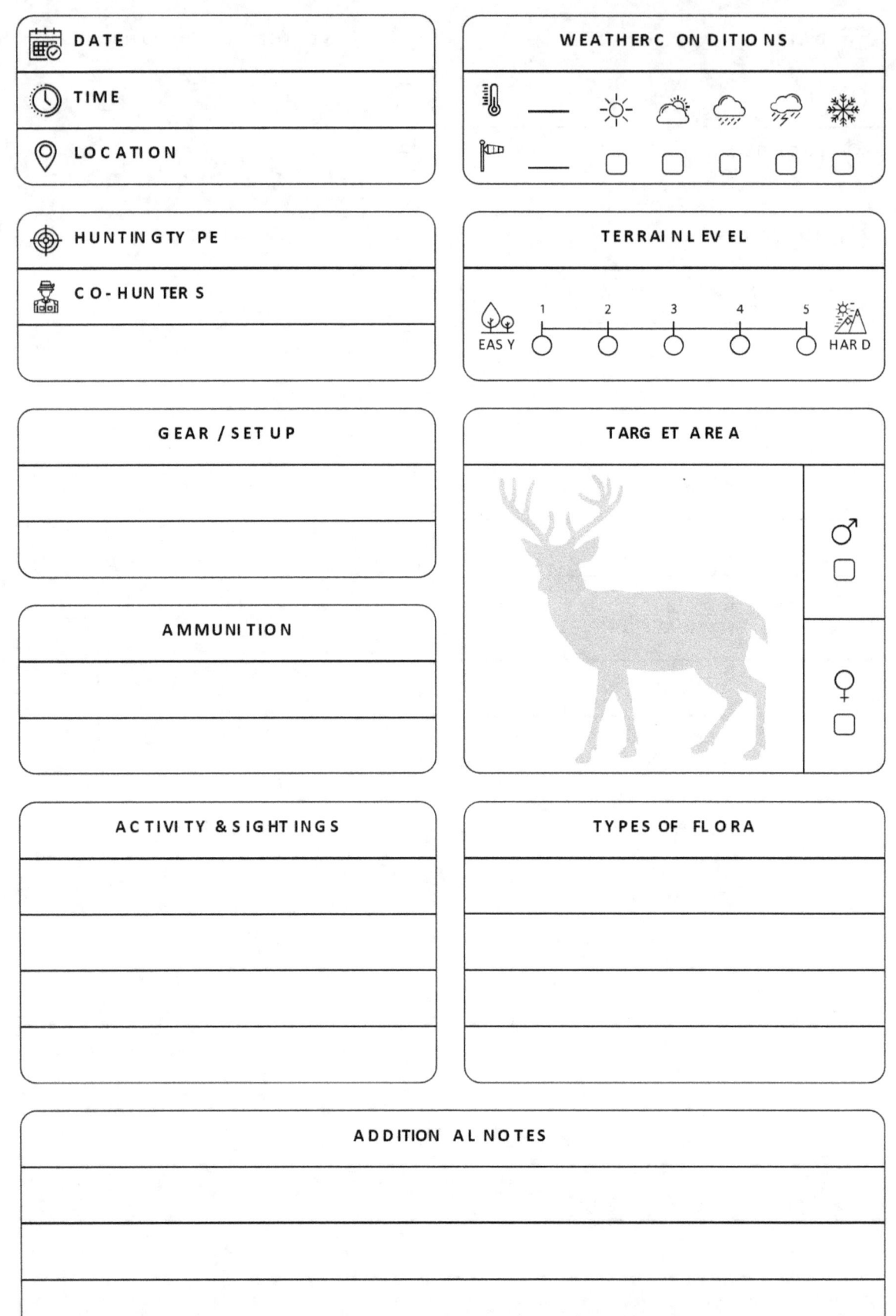

Hunting Log

- **DATE**
- **TIME**
- **LOCATION**

WEATHER CONDITIONS
🌡 _____ ☀ ☁ 🌧 ⛈ ❄
🚩 _____ ☐ ☐ ☐ ☐ ☐

- **HUNTING TYPE**
- **CO-HUNTERS**

TERRAIN LEVEL
EASY 1 ○ 2 ○ 3 ○ 4 ○ 5 ○ HARD

GEAR / SETUP

AMMUNITION

TARGET AREA
♂ ☐
♀ ☐

ACTIVITY & SIGHTINGS

TYPES OF FLORA

ADDITIONAL NOTES

DATE
TIME
LOCATION

WEATHER CONDITIONS

HUNTING TYPE
CO-HUNTERS

TERRAIN LEVEL

1 — 2 — 3 — 4 — 5
EASY ○ ○ ○ ○ ○ HARD

GEAR / SETUP

TARGET AREA

♂ ☐

♀ ☐

AMMUNITION

ACTIVITY & SIGHTINGS

TYPES OF FLORA

ADDITIONAL NOTES

DATE	WEATHER CONDITIONS
TIME	🌡 ___ ☀ ⛅ 🌧 ⛈ ❄
LOCATION	🚩 ___ ☐ ☐ ☐ ☐ ☐

HUNTING TYPE

CO-HUNTERS

TERRAIN LEVEL

EASY 1 2 3 4 5 HARD

GEAR / SETUP

TARGET AREA

♂ ☐

♀ ☐

AMMUNITION

ACTIVITY & SIGHTINGS

TYPES OF FLORA

ADDITIONAL NOTES

DATE
TIME
LOCATION

HUNTING TYPE
CO-HUNTERS

GEAR / SETUP

AMMUNITION

ACTIVITY & SIGHTINGS

WEATHER CONDITIONS

TERRAIN LEVEL

EASY 1 2 3 4 5 HARD

TARGET AREA

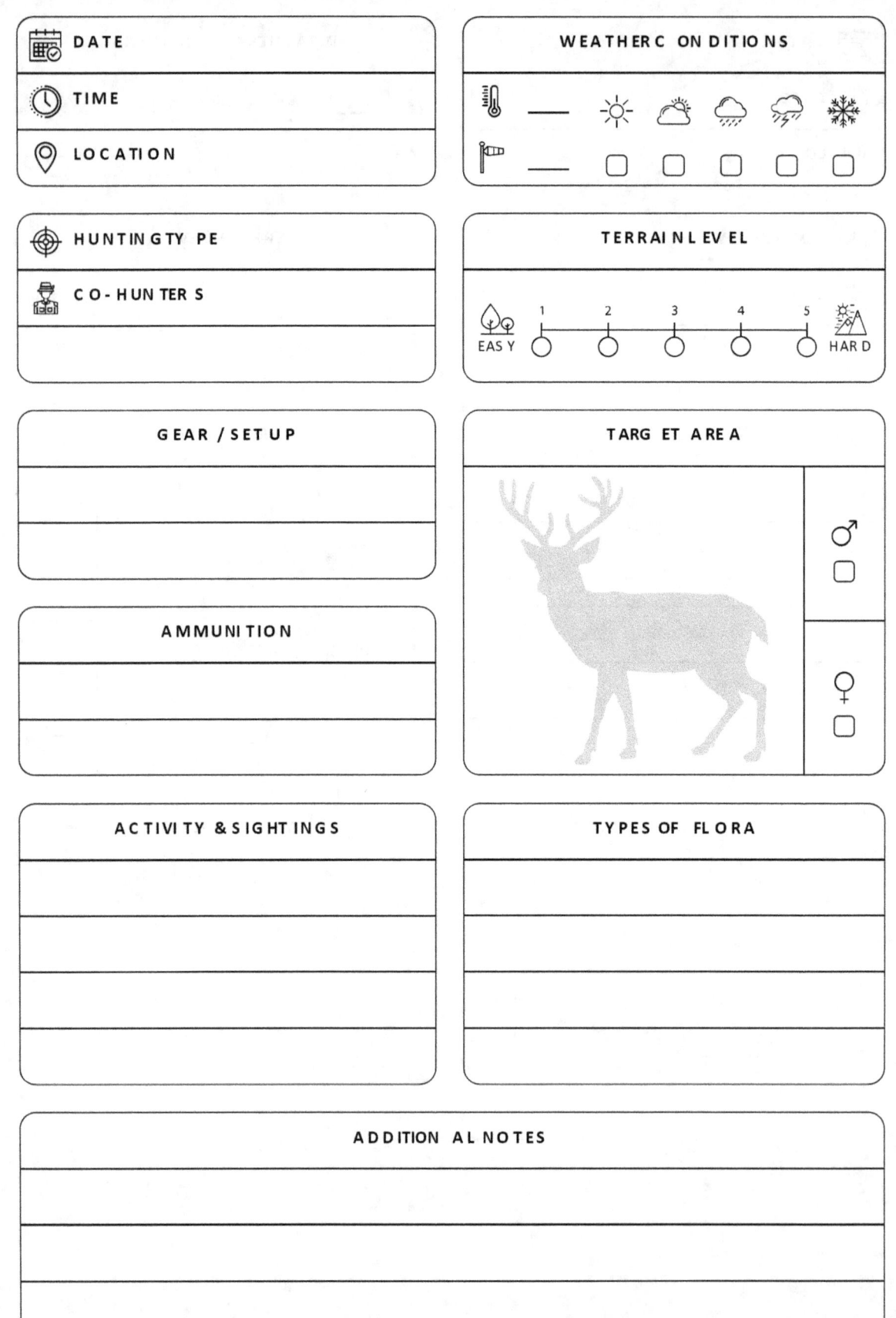

♂
♀

TYPES OF FLORA

ADDITIONAL NOTES

DATE	WEATHER CONDITIONS
TIME	
LOCATION	

HUNTING TYPE	TERRAIN LEVEL
CO-HUNTERS	EASY 1 2 3 4 5 HARD

GEAR / SETUP

TARGET AREA

♂ ☐
♀ ☐

AMMUNITION

ACTIVITY & SIGHTINGS

TYPES OF FLORA

ADDITIONAL NOTES

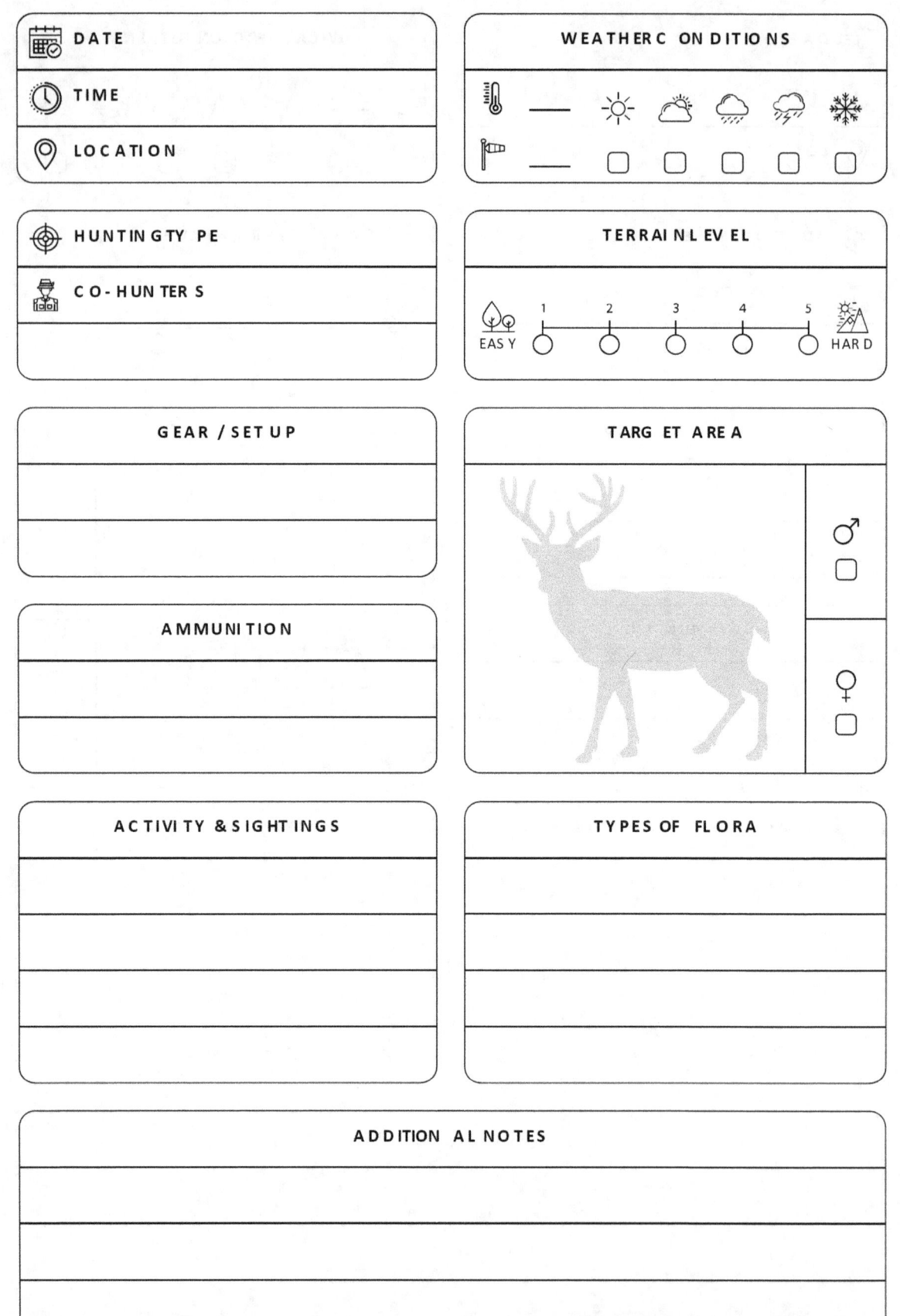

DATE	WEATHER CONDITIONS
TIME	☀️ ⛅ 🌧️ ⛈️ ❄️
LOCATION	☐ ☐ ☐ ☐ ☐

HUNTING TYPE
CO-HUNTERS

TERRAIN LEVEL
EASY 1 2 3 4 5 HARD

GEAR / SETUP

TARGET AREA
♂ ☐
♀ ☐

AMMUNITION

ACTIVITY & SIGHTINGS

TYPES OF FLORA

ADDITIONAL NOTES

DATE	WEATHER CONDITIONS
TIME	
LOCATION	

HUNTING TYPE	TERRAIN LEVEL
CO-HUNTERS	EASY 1 2 3 4 5 HARD

GEAR / SETUP	TARGET AREA
AMMUNITION	♂ ♀

ACTIVITY & SIGHTINGS	TYPES OF FLORA

ADDITIONAL NOTES

DATE	**WEATHER CONDITIONS**
TIME	☀️ ⛅ 🌧️ ⛈️ ❄️
LOCATION	☐ ☐ ☐ ☐ ☐

HUNTING TYPE	**TERRAIN LEVEL**
CO-HUNTERS	EASY 1—2—3—4—5 HARD

GEAR / SETUP

TARGET AREA

♂ ☐

♀ ☐

AMMUNITION

ACTIVITY & SIGHTINGS

TYPES OF FLORA

ADDITIONAL NOTES

DATE

TIME

LOCATION

HUNTING TYPE

CO-HUNTERS

WEATHER CONDITIONS

TERRAIN LEVEL

EASY 1 2 3 4 5 HARD

GEAR / SETUP

TARGET AREA

♂

♀

AMMUNITION

ACTIVITY & SIGHTINGS

TYPES OF FLORA

ADDITIONAL NOTES

DATE	WEATHER CONDITIONS
TIME	
LOCATION	

HUNTING TYPE	TERRAIN LEVEL
CO-HUNTERS	EASY 1 2 3 4 5 HARD

GEAR / SETUP

TARGET AREA

♂ ☐

♀ ☐

AMMUNITION

ACTIVITY & SIGHTINGS

TYPES OF FLORA

ADDITIONAL NOTES

DATE
TIME
LOCATION

HUNTING TYPE
CO-HUNTERS

WEATHER CONDITIONS
🌡 ____   ☀ ⛅ 🌧 ⛈ ❄
🚩 ____   ☐ ☐ ☐ ☐ ☐

TERRAIN LEVEL
EASY 1 2 3 4 5 HARD

GEAR / SETUP

AMMUNITION

TARGET AREA

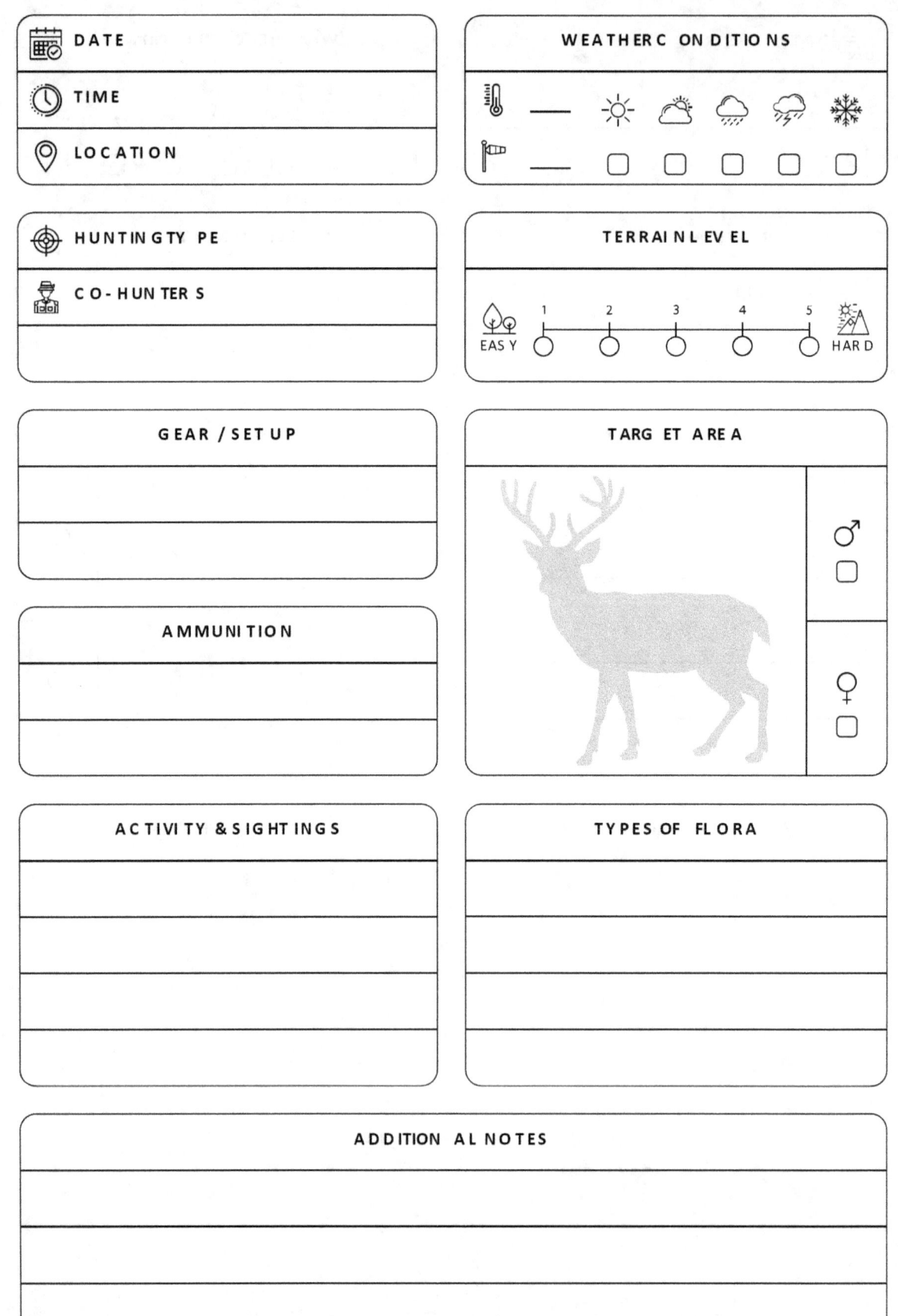

♂ ☐

♀ ☐

ACTIVITY & SIGHTINGS

TYPES OF FLORA

ADDITIONAL NOTES

DATE	WEATHER CONDITIONS
TIME	☀ ⛅ 🌧 ⛈ ❄
LOCATION	☐ ☐ ☐ ☐ ☐

HUNTING TYPE
CO-HUNTERS

TERRAIN LEVEL

EASY 1 2 3 4 5 HARD

GEAR / SETUP

TARGET AREA

♂ ☐

♀ ☐

AMMUNITION

ACTIVITY & SIGHTINGS

TYPES OF FLORA

ADDITIONAL NOTES

DATE	WEATHER CONDITIONS
TIME	
LOCATION	

HUNTING TYPE	TERRAIN LEVEL
CO-HUNTERS	EASY 1 2 3 4 5 HARD

GEAR / SETUP	TARGET AREA
	♂
AMMUNITION	♀

ACTIVITY & SIGHTINGS	TYPES OF FLORA

ADDITIONAL NOTES

DATE
TIME
LOCATION

WEATHER CONDITIONS

🌡 ———   ☀ ⛅ 🌧 ⛈ ❄
🚩 ———   ☐ ☐ ☐ ☐ ☐

HUNTING TYPE
CO-HUNTERS

TERRAIN LEVEL

EASY 1 — 2 — 3 — 4 — 5 HARD

GEAR / SETUP

TARGET AREA

♂ ☐

♀ ☐

AMMUNITION

ACTIVITY & SIGHTINGS

TYPES OF FLORA

ADDITIONAL NOTES

DATE	WEATHER CONDITIONS
TIME	☀️ ⛅ ☁️ 🌧️ ❄️
LOCATION	🌬️ ☐ ☐ ☐ ☐ ☐

HUNTING TYPE	TERRAIN LEVEL
CO-HUNTERS	EASY 1 — 2 — 3 — 4 — 5 HARD

GEAR / SETUP

TARGET AREA

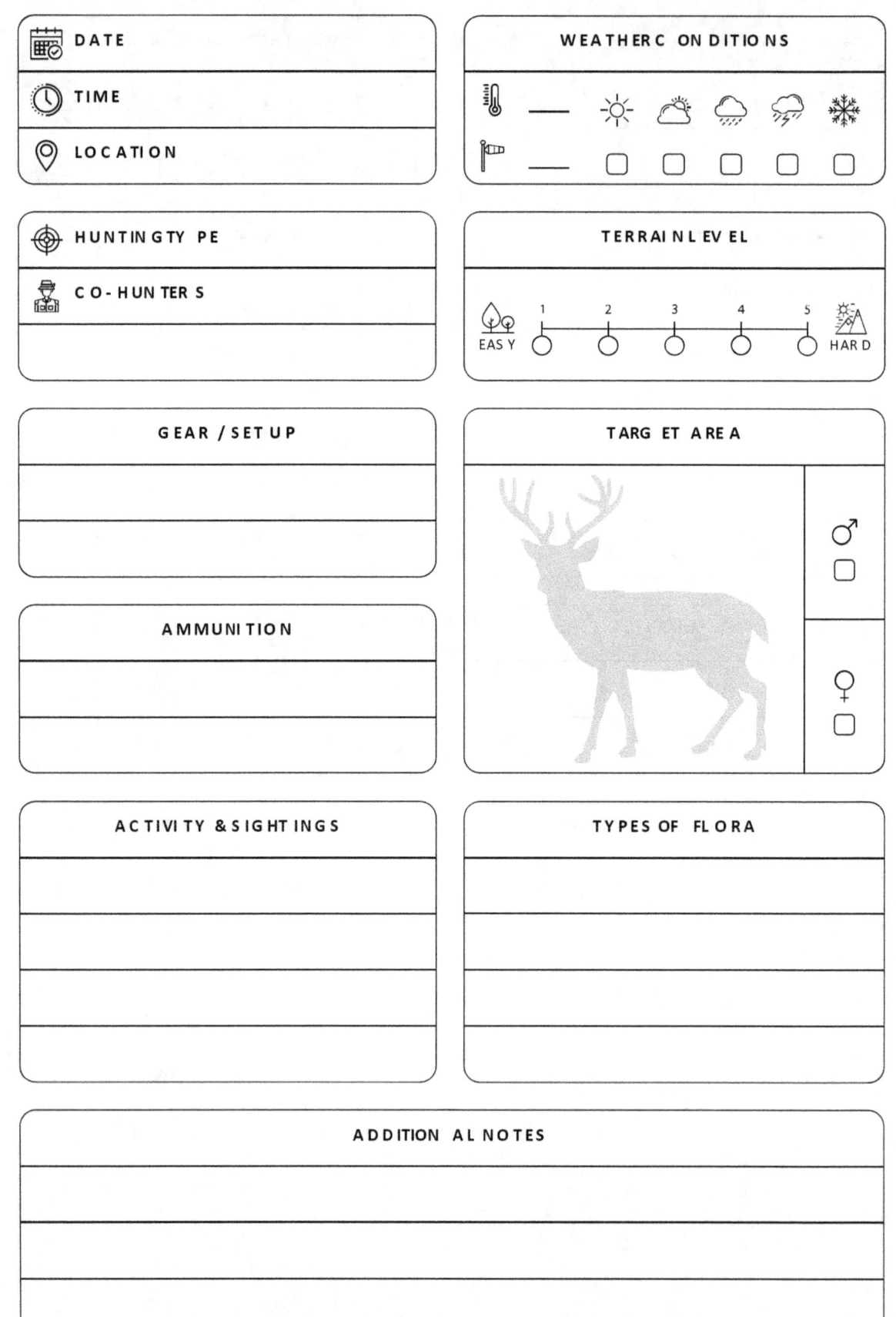

♂ ☐

♀ ☐

AMMUNITION

ACTIVITY & SIGHTINGS

TYPES OF FLORA

ADDITIONAL NOTES

DATE	WEATHER CONDITIONS
TIME	
LOCATION	

HUNTING TYPE	TERRAIN LEVEL
CO-HUNTERS	EASY 1 2 3 4 5 HARD

GEAR / SETUP	TARGET AREA
AMMUNITION	♂ ♀

ACTIVITY & SIGHTINGS	TYPES OF FLORA

ADDITIONAL NOTES

📅 DATE	
🕐 TIME	
📍 LOCATION	

WEATHER CONDITIONS

🌡️ _____ ☀️ ⛅ 🌧️ ⛈️ ❄️

🎐 _____ ☐ ☐ ☐ ☐ ☐

🎯 HUNTING TYPE	
🪖 CO-HUNTERS	

TERRAIN LEVEL

🌳 EASY 1 ○ 2 ○ 3 ○ 4 ○ 5 ○ ⛰️ HARD

GEAR / SETUP

AMMUNITION

TARGET AREA

♂ ☐

♀ ☐

ACTIVITY & SIGHTINGS

TYPES OF FLORA

ADDITIONAL NOTES

DATE	WEATHER CONDITIONS
TIME	
LOCATION	

HUNTING TYPE	TERRAIN LEVEL
CO-HUNTERS	1 2 3 4 5 — EASY / HARD

GEAR / SETUP	TARGET AREA
	♂
AMMUNITION	♀

ACTIVITY & SIGHTINGS	TYPES OF FLORA

ADDITIONAL NOTES

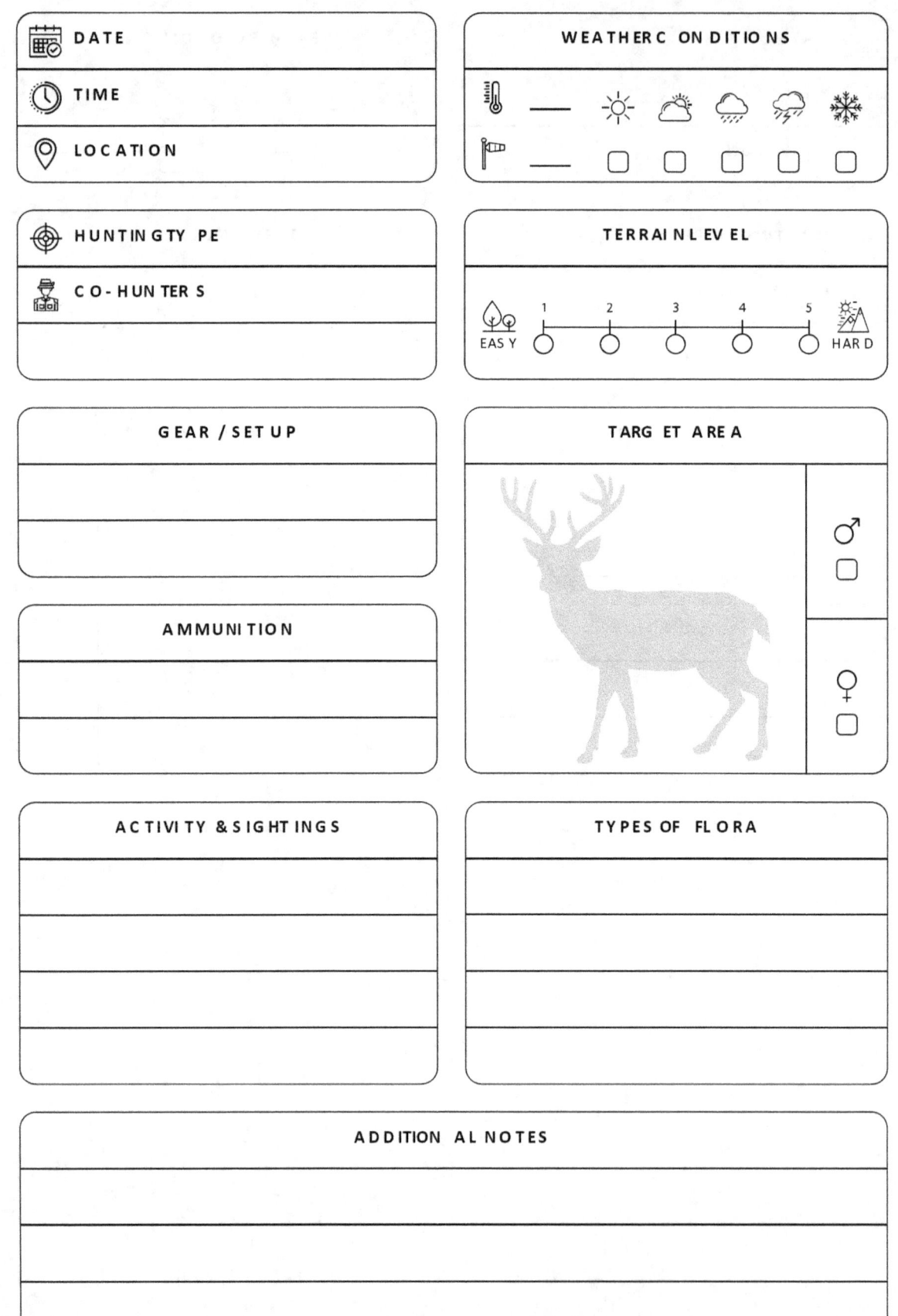

DATE	
TIME	
LOCATION	

HUNTING TYPE	
CO-HUNTERS	

WEATHER CONDITIONS

TERRAIN LEVEL

EASY 1 2 3 4 5 HARD

GEAR / SETUP

AMMUNITION

TARGET AREA

♂
♀

ACTIVITY & SIGHTINGS

TYPES OF FLORA

ADDITIONAL NOTES

DATE	WEATHER CONDITIONS
TIME	
LOCATION	

HUNTING TYPE

CO-HUNTERS

TERRAIN LEVEL

EASY 1 2 3 4 5 HARD

GEAR / SETUP

TARGET AREA

♂ ☐

♀ ☐

AMMUNITION

ACTIVITY & SIGHTINGS

TYPES OF FLORA

ADDITIONAL NOTES

DATE	WEATHER CONDITIONS
TIME	
LOCATION	

HUNTING TYPE	TERRAIN LEVEL
CO-HUNTERS	EASY 1 2 3 4 5 HARD

GEAR / SETUP	TARGET AREA
AMMUNITION	♂ ♀

ACTIVITY & SIGHTINGS	TYPES OF FLORA

ADDITIONAL NOTES

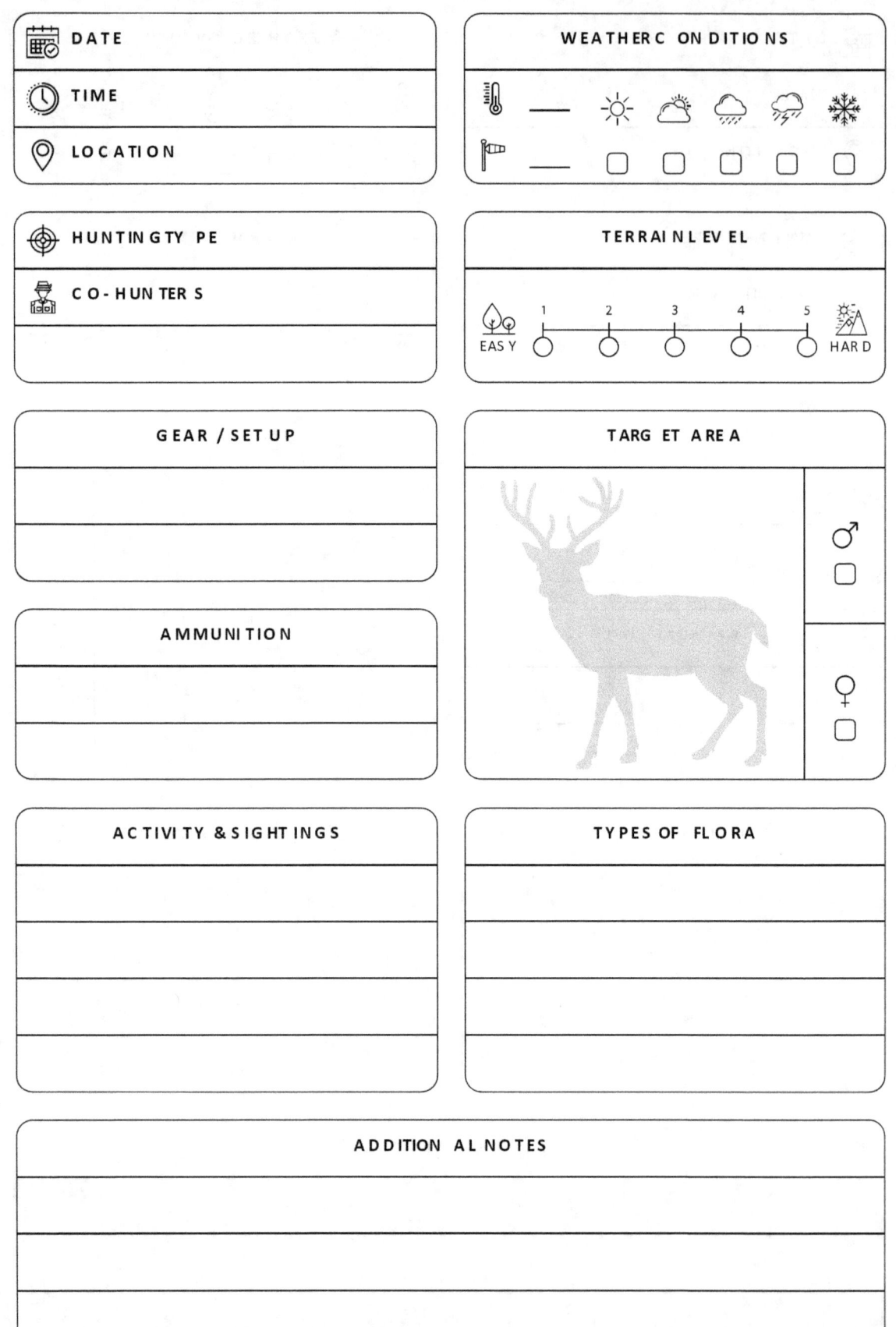

DATE	**WEATHER CONDITIONS**
TIME	
LOCATION	

- DATE
- TIME
- LOCATION

WEATHER CONDITIONS

HUNTING TYPE

CO-HUNTERS

TERRAIN LEVEL

1   2   3   4   5
EASY ─────────── HARD

GEAR / SETUP

TARGET AREA

♂

♀

AMMUNITION

ACTIVITY & SIGHTINGS

TYPES OF FLORA

ADDITIONAL NOTES

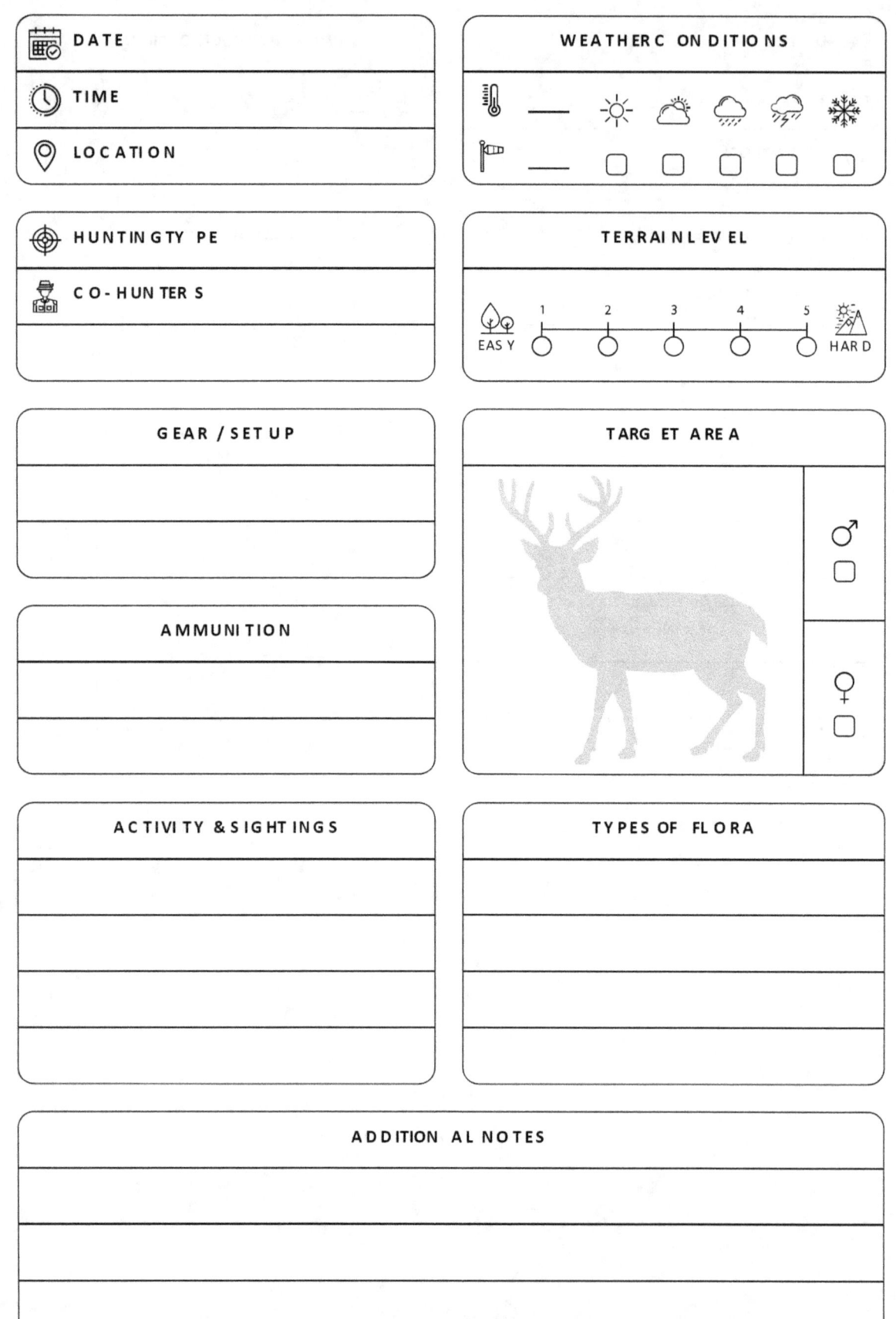

DATE	**WEATHER CONDITIONS**
TIME	☀️ ⛅ 🌧️ ⛈️ ❄️
LOCATION	

HUNTING TYPE	**TERRAIN LEVEL**
CO-HUNTERS	EASY 1 — 2 — 3 — 4 — 5 HARD

GEAR / SETUP

TARGET AREA

♂
♀

AMMUNITION

ACTIVITY & SIGHTINGS

TYPES OF FLORA

ADDITIONAL NOTES

DATE	WEATHER CONDITIONS
TIME	☀️ ⛅ 🌧️ ⛈️ ❄️
LOCATION	☐ ☐ ☐ ☐ ☐

HUNTING TYPE	TERRAIN LEVEL
CO-HUNTERS	EASY 1 2 3 4 5 HARD

GEAR / SETUP

TARGET AREA

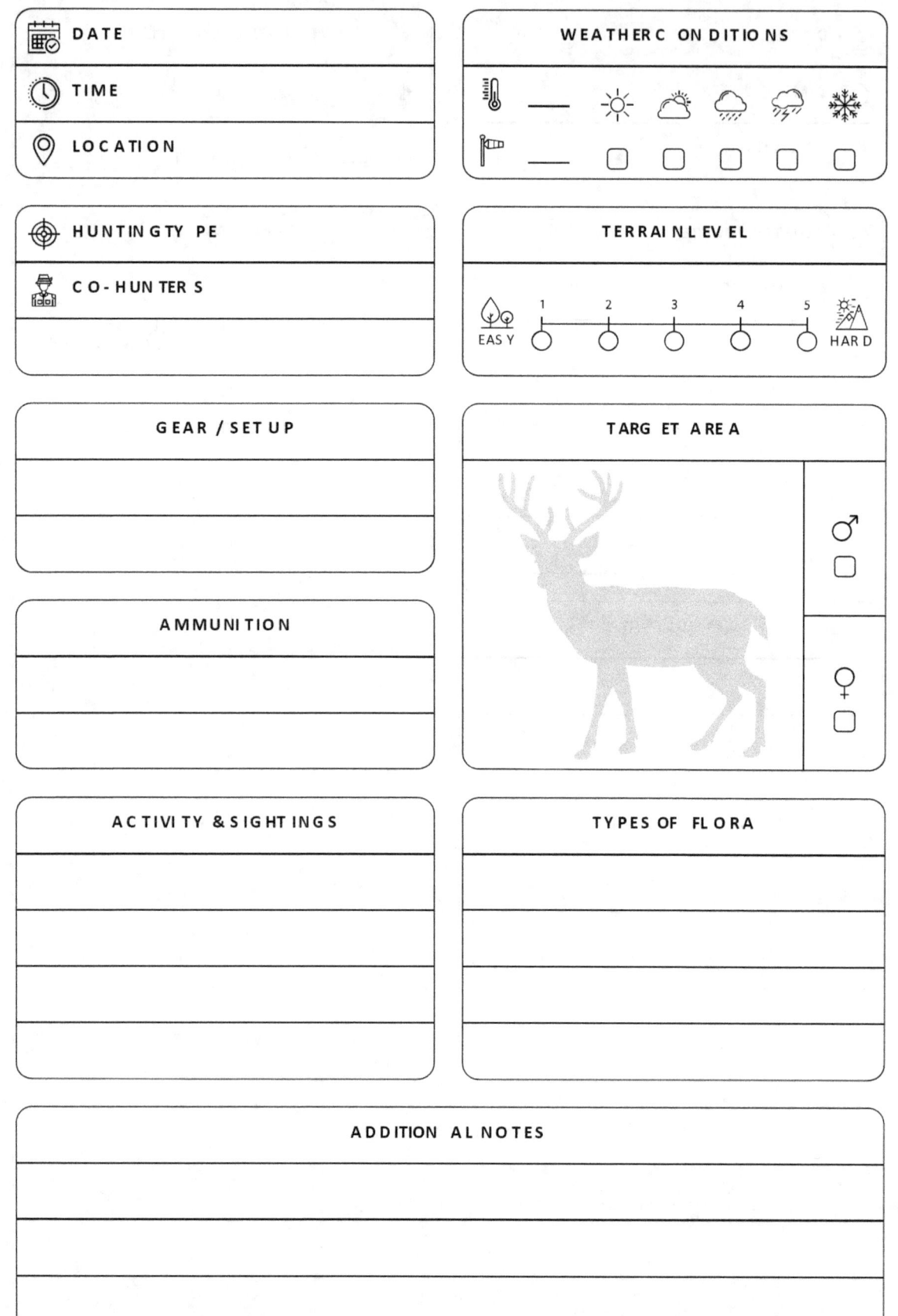

♂ ☐

♀ ☐

AMMUNITION

ACTIVITY & SIGHTINGS

TYPES OF FLORA

ADDITIONAL NOTES

DATE
TIME
LOCATION

HUNTING TYPE
CO-HUNTERS

GEAR / SETUP

AMMUNITION

WEATHER CONDITIONS

TERRAIN LEVEL

EASY 1 2 3 4 5 HARD

TARGET AREA

♂
♀

ACTIVITY & SIGHTINGS

TYPES OF FLORA

ADDITIONAL NOTES

📅 DATE	
🕐 TIME	
📍 LOCATION	

WEATHER CONDITIONS

🌡️ _____ ☀️ ⛅ 🌧️ ⛈️ ❄️
🌬️ _____ ☐ ☐ ☐ ☐ ☐

🎯 HUNTING TYPE
🕵️ CO-HUNTERS

TERRAIN LEVEL

EASY 1 — 2 — 3 — 4 — 5 HARD
      ○   ○   ○   ○   ○

GEAR / SETUP

AMMUNITION

TARGET AREA

♂ ☐

♀ ☐

ACTIVITY & SIGHTINGS

TYPES OF FLORA

ADDITIONAL NOTES

📅 **DATE**	
🕐 **TIME**	
📍 **LOCATION**	

WEATHER CONDITIONS

🌡 _____ ☀️ ⛅ 🌧 ⛈ ❄️
🚩 _____ ☐ ☐ ☐ ☐ ☐

- 🎯 **HUNTING TYPE**
- 👤 **CO-HUNTERS**

TERRAIN LEVEL

EASY 1 — 2 — 3 — 4 — 5 HARD
       ○   ○   ○   ○   ○

GEAR / SETUP

TARGET AREA

♂ ☐

♀ ☐

AMMUNITION

ACTIVITY & SIGHTINGS

TYPES OF FLORA

ADDITIONAL NOTES

DATE	WEATHER CONDITIONS
TIME	☀ ⛅ 🌧 ⛈ ❄
LOCATION	☐ ☐ ☐ ☐ ☐

HUNTING TYPE	TERRAIN LEVEL
CO-HUNTERS	EASY 1 — 2 — 3 — 4 — 5 HARD

GEAR / SETUP

TARGET AREA

♂ ☐

♀ ☐

AMMUNITION

ACTIVITY & SIGHTINGS

TYPES OF FLORA

ADDITIONAL NOTES

DATE	WEATHER CONDITIONS
TIME	
LOCATION	

HUNTING TYPE	TERRAIN LEVEL
CO-HUNTERS	1 2 3 4 5
	EASY ○ ○ ○ ○ ○ HARD

GEAR / SETUP

TARGET AREA

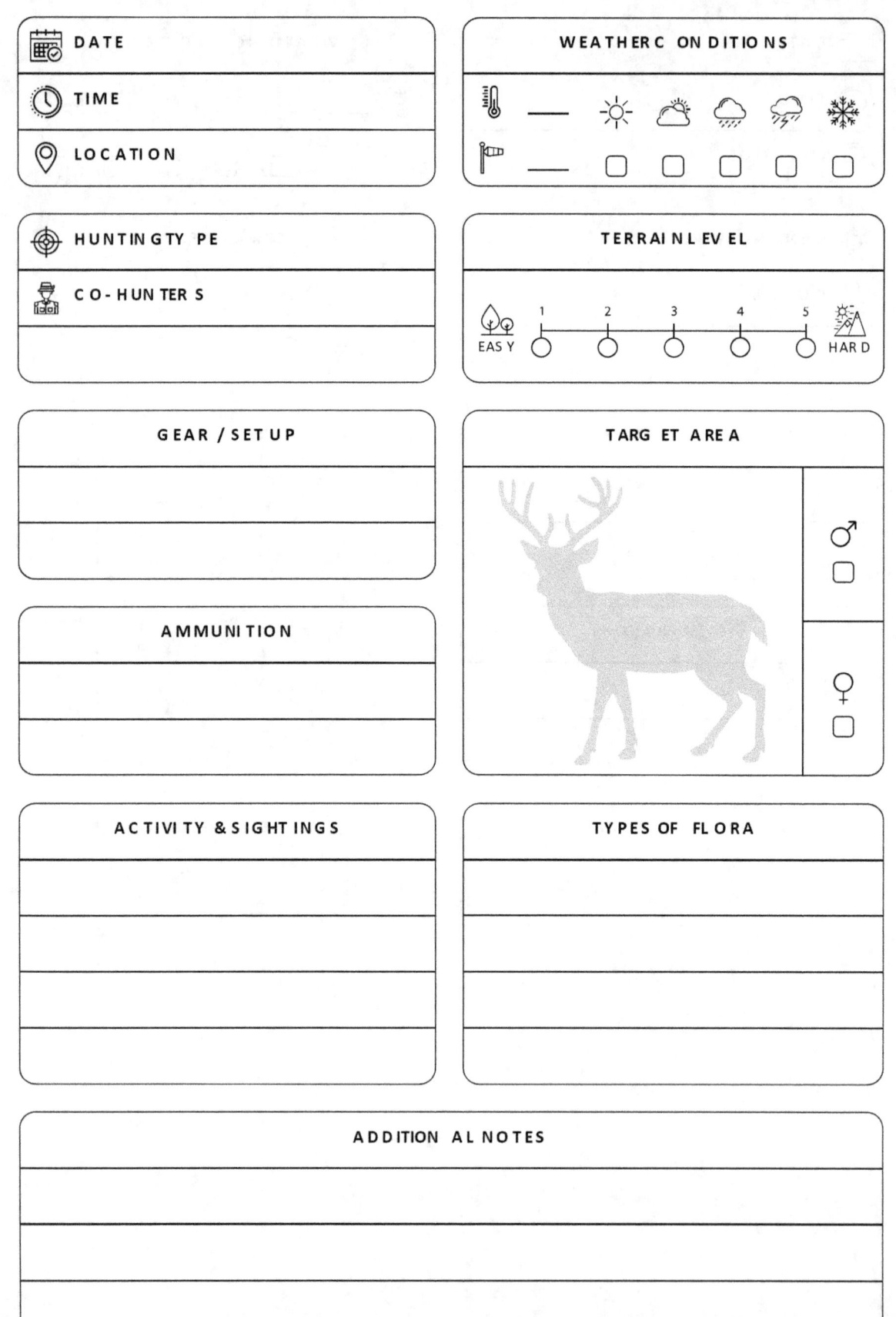

♂ ☐

♀ ☐

AMMUNITION

ACTIVITY & SIGHTINGS

TYPES OF FLORA

ADDITIONAL NOTES

DATE	WEATHER CONDITIONS
TIME	☀ ⛅ 🌧 ⛈ ❄
LOCATION	☐ ☐ ☐ ☐ ☐

HUNTING TYPE

CO-HUNTERS

TERRAIN LEVEL

EASY 1 2 3 4 5 HARD

GEAR / SETUP

TARGET AREA

♂ ☐

♀ ☐

AMMUNITION

ACTIVITY & SIGHTINGS

TYPES OF FLORA

ADDITIONAL NOTES

DATE	WEATHER CONDITIONS
TIME	
LOCATION	

HUNTING TYPE	TERRAIN LEVEL
CO-HUNTERS	EASY 1 2 3 4 5 HARD

GEAR / SETUP	TARGET AREA
AMMUNITION	♂ / ♀

ACTIVITY & SIGHTINGS	TYPES OF FLORA

ADDITIONAL NOTES

DATE
TIME
LOCATION

WEATHER CONDITIONS

HUNTING TYPE

CO-HUNTERS

TERRAIN LEVEL

EASY 1 2 3 4 5 HARD

GEAR / SETUP

TARGET AREA

♂

♀

AMMUNITION

ACTIVITY & SIGHTINGS

TYPES OF FLORA

ADDITIONAL NOTES

DATE	WEATHER CONDITIONS
TIME	
LOCATION	

HUNTING TYPE	TERRAIN LEVEL
CO-HUNTERS	EASY 1 2 3 4 5 HARD

GEAR / SETUP	TARGET AREA
	♂
AMMUNITION	♀

ACTIVITY & SIGHTINGS	TYPES OF FLORA

ADDITIONAL NOTES

DATE	WEATHER CONDITIONS
TIME	
LOCATION	

HUNTING TYPE	TERRAIN LEVEL
CO-HUNTERS	EASY 1 2 3 4 5 HARD

GEAR / SETUP	TARGET AREA
AMMUNITION	♂ ♀

ACTIVITY & SIGHTINGS	TYPES OF FLORA

ADDITIONAL NOTES

DATE	WEATHER CONDITIONS
TIME	
LOCATION	

HUNTING TYPE	TERRAIN LEVEL
CO-HUNTERS	EASY 1 2 3 4 5 HARD

GEAR / SETUP	TARGET AREA
AMMUNITION	♂ / ♀

ACTIVITY & SIGHTINGS	TYPES OF FLORA

ADDITIONAL NOTES

📅 DATE	
🕐 TIME	
📍 LOCATION	

WEATHER CONDITIONS

🌡 _____ ☀️ ⛅ 🌧 ⛈ ❄️
🪁 _____ ☐ ☐ ☐ ☐ ☐

🎯 HUNTING TYPE	
🧑‍🌾 CO-HUNTERS	

TERRAIN LEVEL

EASY 1 2 3 4 5 HARD

GEAR / SETUP

AMMUNITION

TARGET AREA

♂ ☐

♀ ☐

ACTIVITY & SIGHTINGS

TYPES OF FLORA

ADDITIONAL NOTES

DATE	WEATHER CONDITIONS
TIME	
LOCATION	

HUNTING TYPE	TERRAIN LEVEL
CO-HUNTERS	EASY 1 2 3 4 5 HARD

GEAR / SETUP

TARGET AREA

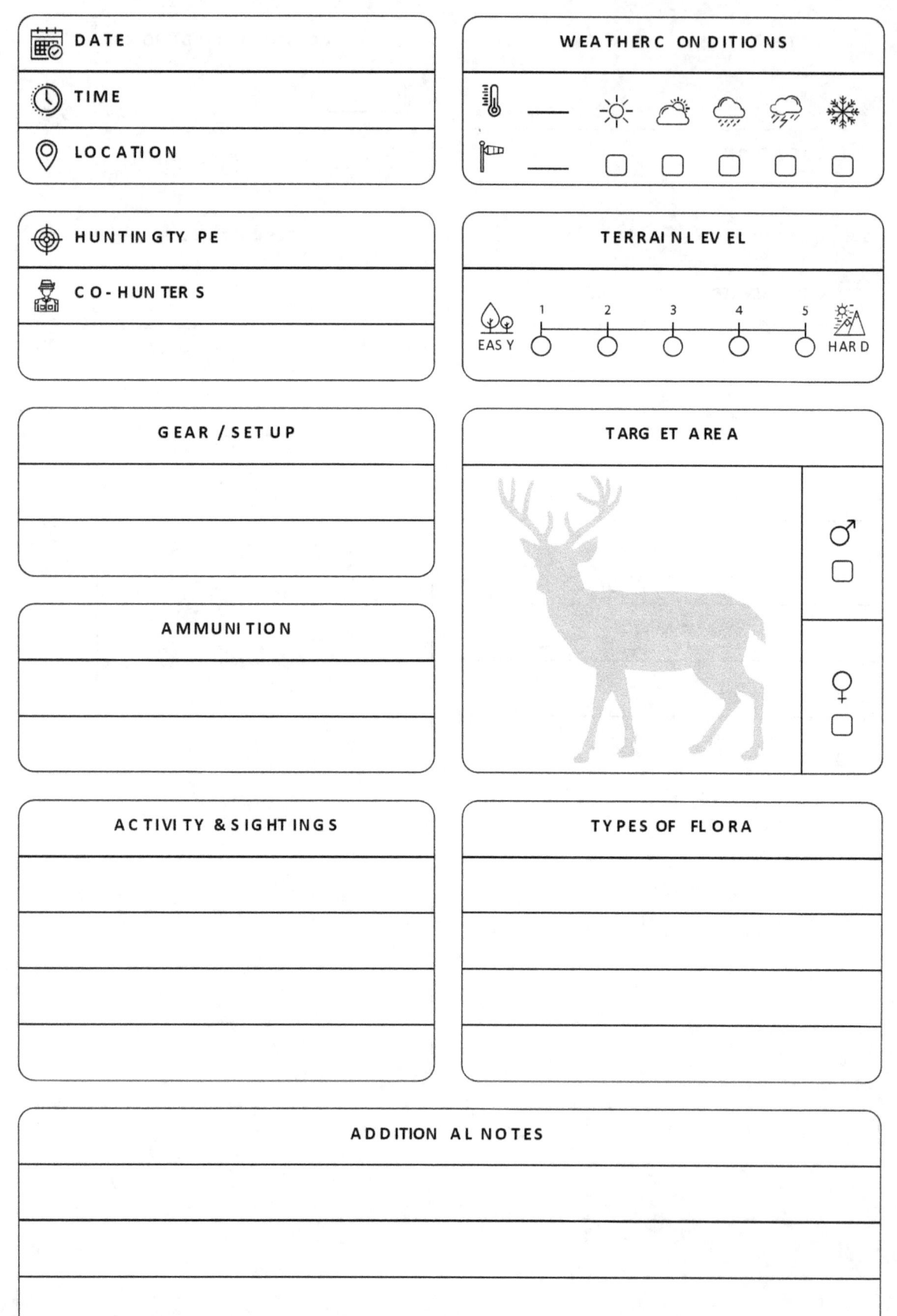

♂ ☐

♀ ☐

AMMUNITION

ACTIVITY & SIGHTINGS

TYPES OF FLORA

ADDITIONAL NOTES

www.ingramcontent.com/pod-product-compliance
Lightning Source LLC
Chambersburg PA
CBHW081155070526
44583CB00021B/2852